WHAT PEOPLE SAY

"Terry's journey is not only an inspiration, but is also a road map to a successful career in IT. Having trained thousands in our IT Engineer Academy and utilizing insights conveyed in this book, I can honestly say *Zero to Engineer* can serve as a beacon for all aspiring IT professionals."
— **Jacob Hess**, Cofounder, NGT Academy

"As a national cybersecurity training academy, there is a certain level of urgency in keeping our country safe. NexGenT's core values are grounded in making a positive difference in the lives of everyday Americans through innovative training systems and hands-on applications. Transitioning veterans looking for their next career are finding fulfilling opportunities after graduation at NexGenT's Phoenix-based campus. As cyberthreats continue to multiply, NexGenT is dedicated to providing cutting-edge innovations and solutions focused on the unmet threats aimed at the United States every day."
— **Military Makeover**

"NexGenT provides real-world IT engineer training that makes students job-ready (for IT Ops roles like network/systems engineer) in months instead of years, and without the typical student debt from traditional institutions."
— **Y Combinator**

"San Jose start-up offers faster, cheaper training for the IT jobs of the future."
— **Silicon Valley Business Journal**

T0278166

ZERO TO ENGINEER

ZERO TO ENGINEER

THE UNCONVENTIONAL BLUEPRINT TO SECURING A 6-FIGURE TECH CAREER

TERRY KIM

WILEY

Published by John Wiley & Sons, Inc., Hoboken, New Jersey.
Published simultaneously in Canada.

For general information on our other products and services or for technical support, please contact our Customer Care Department within the United States at (800) 762-2974, outside the United States at (317) 572-3993 or fax (317) 572-4002.

Wiley also publishes its books in a variety of electronic formats. Some content that appears in print may not be available in electronic formats. For more information about Wiley products, visit our web site at www.wiley.com.

Library of Congress Control Number: 2024950282

Paperback ISBN: 9781394297849

ePDF ISBN: 9781394297863

ePUB ISBN: 9781394297856

Cover Image: Wiley

Cover Design: Wiley

Set in 11/16pt MinionPro by Lumina Datamatics

SKY10094033_121724

CONTENTS

CONTENTS

BONUS

By purchasing this book you get access to these three amazing bonuses!

Bonus 1: CompTIA Network+ (FREE)

You'll get unlimited access to the CompTIA Network+ Certification Course, which will help you stand out in the fast-paced IT industry. This course teaches you important skills like troubleshooting, configuring, and managing networks and devices.

Bonus 2: Career Strategy Session (FREE)

You'll receive a one-on-one career strategy session with our highly skilled IT career specialists. We understand that navigating the job market and advancing your career can be tough, but with our expert guidance, you'll have the tools to achieve your goals and secure the bright future you deserve.

Bonus 3: ZERO TO ENGINEER Community (FREE)

We're excited to present you with an exclusive invitation to join our Zero to Engineer Community Group. This is your opportunity to connect with like-minded individuals who are embarking on the same IT journey as you.

Do you have an audience that could benefit from this book?

Bulk Discounts and Promotional links available. Submit an email to info@nexgent.com with your request and we will be in touch.

FOREWORD

I n a world where digital threats know no boundaries, the need for cybersecurity warriors to safeguard our nation has never been more critical. As someone who has dedicated 30 years of their life to defending our country's cyberspace, I understand the immense importance of staying ahead in the cybersecurity  realm. Terry Kim and Jacob Hess, co-founders of NGT Academy, share this commitment to securing our nation's digital future.

Zero to Engineer is a game-changing book that not only outlines the path to landing your dream IT or cyber job without a college degree but also emphasizes the vital role these individuals play in maintaining our nation's security. The NGT Academy program, which Terry and Jacob have meticulously crafted, offers military-grade training that equips students with the skills and knowledge necessary to excel in the cybersecurity landscape. Their dedication to excellence is unmatched, making their academy the best choice for aspiring IT professionals.

I am thrilled to support Terry Kim's mission through this foreword. Together, we can empower a new generation of IT professionals, providing them with the tools they need to protect our country against evolving digital threats. As veterans and cybersecurity enthusiasts, we understand the importance of preparedness and resilience, and NGT Academy embodies these values at every step.

Anthony Thomas

Former Director of U.S. Air Force Cyberspace Operations

Founder & Principal

Tony Thomas & Associates LLC & Quadrant Four

GI BILL APPROVAL

G I Bill ApprovalAt NGT Academy, we are proud to offer our Full Stack Network Engineer & Cybersecurity Accelerator program in partnership with International American University (IAU), enabling veterans to utilize their GI Bill® benefits for enrollment. This approval enables us to provide accessible and high-quality training to those who have served our country, helping them unlock new opportunities in the tech industry. By equipping veterans with the skills needed to excel in the tech industry, we're honored to play a part in shaping their futures and contributing to their continued success.

Apply here: https://ngt.academy/veterans/

ABOUT THE AUTHOR

Terry Kim, a veteran of the U.S. Air Force and a first-generation Korean American, boasts a career spanning more than two decades in the field of IT. Beginning with a classified top secret clearance during his military service, he ascended through the ranks at prominent tech giants such as Cisco Systems and Arista Networks. His journey underscores that achieving mastery in engineering doesn't necessarily demand years of conventional education. Instead, he embarked on a mission to revolutionize IT learning, emphasizing practical skill development with mentorship to swiftly prepare individuals for employment within a span of four months, as opposed to the traditional four-year route.

As the Founder of NGT Academy and an alumnus of YCombinator, Terry has garnered an impressive $18 million in venture capital from distinguished sources in Silicon Valley. NGT Academy's overarching goal is to cultivate one million proficient IT professionals by the year 2030. Terry also interweaves spiritual insights into his pedagogy, motivating learners to not only shape the realm of technology but also to mold their own destinies. This approach is firmly grounded in the transformative principles of Kaizen, a Japanese term embodying "positive change" and "continuous improvement."

ACKNOWLEDGMENTS

First and foremost, to my remarkable mother, your journey and sacrifices have shaped me into the person I am today. From the shores of Jindo Island to the bustling streets of Seoul and eventually to the United States, your resilience and determination inspire me daily. Your belief in my potential, even when I doubted myself, has fueled my drive to succeed. Thank you for being my guiding light.

I want to express my deepest gratitude to Jacob Hess for his years of dedicated service and tireless efforts that have been pivotal to NGT Academy's growth and success. Your contributions have played a vital role in shaping our mission to empower aspiring engineers and redefine education. Thank you for being part of this journey and for the impact you've made along the way.

I extend my heartfelt appreciation to the incredible team at NGT Academy. Your passion, expertise, and commitment are the driving force behind our mission. Together, we're empowering individuals to realize their dreams and forge new paths in the IT industry. Your dedication to our students' success is immeasurable, and I am grateful for each of you.

Lastly, a special thank-you to our students and readers, who inspire me with your determination to learn and grow. Your journey is a testament to the transformative power of education and the boundless opportunities that await in the world of IT. Your success fuels our purpose, and I'm honored to be a part of your journey.

With immense gratitude,

Terry Kim

Founder/CEO of NGT Academy

INTRODUCTION

A t 31 years old, I was employed as a systems engineer (architect) at Cisco Systems, a Fortune 100 tech company. It's a job that exceeded my wildest dreams in terms of the income it provided. Sometimes, I had to pinch myself to make sure it wasn't all just a dream. In fact, I have a picture of one of my first paychecks from Cisco, which was nearly $10,000 for just two weeks of work.

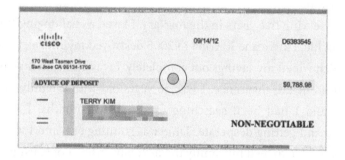

Landing that IT job, which had always been my dream, seemed almost effortless, thanks to the secrets and strategies that I will share with you later in this book.

What's truly astonishing is that I achieved all this with just an eighth-grade education and as a first-generation Korean American immigrant. This goes to show that you don't have to have an expensive college degree to break into the field of information technology. I obtained my high school diploma by passing the GED in order to join the U.S. Air Force. I joined in 1999, just before the dotcom bubble and right when the movie *The Matrix* was released. At the age of 21, seeing that movie ignited a passion within me for computers and all things technology. Prior to that, I didn't even know how to operate a PC. But once I saw what was possible, I was hooked. I instantly realized that this was the future, and I was determined to be a part of the tech boom revolution. I knew I had to learn this technology or risk being left behind. So, I built my first PC, and that was the beginning of an incredible journey.

This mindset of going from nothing to something of value is key when starting any career or learning new skills. Instead of being afraid of failure, all it took was the willpower to say, "This is what I'm going to do, and I'm going to figure it out one step at a time." That's exactly what I did, and along the way, I discovered many secrets and industry insights that will save you tons of time, money, and energy, accelerating your path to landing your dream IT job.

After serving five years in the military, I faced a challenging transition to civilian life. Hurricane Katrina in 2005 destroyed my Internet cafe business, which wiped my savings out completely. I was broke, in massive debt, and had no health insurance. I was 26 years old with a family of four to support, and I had been searching for a job for months. I was pretty depressed and getting desperate. Time was running out, and I was afraid I wouldn't be able to feed my family the next day. Instead of fearing failure, I had to take action immediately. With my acquired IT skills from my time in the Air Force, I knew I had the potential to work for Cisco Systems. So, together with my wife, who was my rock during that difficult time, I created a plan to land my first civilian IT job. After much perseverance, I secured an entry-level IT position as a network technician at a local credit union, earning a modest salary of $28,000 per year. But that was just the beginning.

In the upcoming chapters, I will share with you the secrets, strategies, and frameworks that allowed me to increase my income from $28,000 to six figures within just two years. And learning from me, most students get huge pay bumps in much less time. Eventually, I even received job offers ranging from $200,000 to $350,000 from top tech companies within five years of starting my civilian career. With this book, I'll give you all the insights I learned so you too can become a six-figure earner.

Today, the time to dive into the field of IT has never been better. With advancements in AI, voice, video, Internet of Things (IoT), blockchain, Web3, the cloud, and the rise of cybersecurity threats, there is a tremendous need for the next generation of IT professionals. In fact, there are approximately 500,000 open IT/cybersecurity jobs in the United States alone as of September 2024 (www.cybersecuritydive.com/news/white-hou se-cybersecurity-500000-job/726162), with an average IT salary of $211,856, which is four times the average salary for all occupations! The rise of AI and automation will create even more opportunities in the technology field over the next decade. Clearly, the time is now for you to jump into the technology industry.

After leaving Cisco Systems and moving on to my next dream job at Arista Networks, I was shocked to see that many people were still struggling to break into the IT field despite spending tens of thousands of dollars on a four-year college degree. In 2015, I created a free course on Udemy titled "How to Become a Cisco Engineer Earning Six Figures." The course received an overwhelming response with numerous thank-you emails and five-star reviews. I knew then that I wanted to make an even greater impact on a much larger scale. I realized that the current college education system is completely broken. The tipping point came when I discovered that private colleges like ITT Technical Institute was charging $80,000 for a bachelor's degree, and I knew then it was a complete scam. In fact, ITT Tech was shut down in 2016. Six years later, the Project on Predatory Lending released a comprehensive report exposing the abuses by ITT, detailing how they defrauded millions of students, leaving them burdened with student loan debt and worthless credentials.

It was at this point that NexGenT, now known as NGT Academy, was born. Together with Jacob Hess, my co-founder and loyal friend, our mission is to revolutionize the way people enter the IT field, taking them from Zero to Engineer in less than four months instead of four years of college.

With this book, whether you choose to train with us at NGT Academy or pursue the journey on your own, you will find everything you need to break into the IT industry. The blueprint is laid out for you, and it has already helped thousands of people from diverse backgrounds successfully enter the IT industry in a matter of months rather than years. All I ask in return is a five-star testimonial on Amazon after reading the book and once you break in. It will let me know that we are making great progress toward our goal of helping one million people enter the IT ecosystem by 2030. You can find more information about our school and program offerings at the end of this book.

I am thrilled for you as you embark on this IT journey that I know will open up countless doors for you. Whether you choose to remain an engineer, become an IT manager, IT director, CIO, CSO, or even start your own tech company or IT consultancy business one day, the possibilities are limitless.

In gratitude,
Terry Kim
Your Mentor and Coach
Founder/CEO of NGT Academy

CHAPTER ONE

DARE TO DREAM: BELIEVE NO MATTER WHAT

"When it comes to life, the critical thing is whether you take things for granted or take them with gratitude."

— G. K. Chesterton

INTRODUCTION

According to Investopedia, and I agree, the American Dream is the belief that anyone, regardless of where they were born or what class they were born into, can attain their own version of success in a society in which upward mobility is possible for everyone. It's a well-known fact that the American Dream is alive and real, and I'm living proof. As a first-generation Korean American with only an eighth-grade education and no college degree, I became a systems engineer at a Fortune 100 company. This is a miracle because, for most of my life, I didn't even know how to use a computer. Seriously, I didn't have a clue.

Clearly, opportunity is everywhere, and when I got my first taste of technology, I knew it was the future. It doesn't matter if you're in the United States or somewhere else in the world, the information technology (IT) sector is booming. For some perspective: In 1999, there were about 1 million devices connected to the Internet.

The Internet of Things (IoT) is growing exponentially, and ASL Holdings found that there will be 75.44 billion IoT-connected devices worldwide by 2025 (https://aslh.co.uk). That means the number of IoT-connected devices has increased over 75,000 times since 1999!

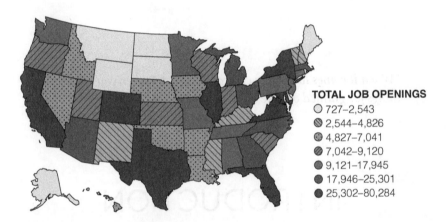

TOTAL JOB OPENINGS
○ 727–2,543
◔ 2,544–4,826
◒ 4,827–7,041
◕ 7,042–9,120
● 9,121–17,945
● 17,946–25,301
● 25,302–80,284

Source: www.cyberseek.org/heatmap.html

That's great, but guess what's tagging along? Cybercrime. It's climbing faster than ever. To throw some numbers at you, in 2021 the United States alone saw damages north of $1 trillion from malicious actors. Industry expert Steve Morgan, editor-in-chief at *Cyber Magazine*, states this could hit a staggering $10 trillion globally by 2025 (https://cybersecurity ventures.com/hackerpocalypse-cybercrime-report-2016). What does this tell us?

We need cyber warriors, and the IT workforce has ever-growing opportunities for skilled workers.

But amidst so much potential and before diving straight into chasing your dreams, there are some things you need to prioritize. First and foremost is gratitude. That's right. To harness the American Dream, and any opportunities for that matter, gratitude is key. Gratitude keeps you grounded and driven. It's the anchor that helps you make the most of these opportunities. You also need the right mindset and to know how to set good habits, creating rituals that give you a rock-solid foundation to build your dream on.

After laying that foundation, I'll give you my highly proven blueprint for manifestation. When you combine gratitude, mindset, habits, and the ability to manifest, everything in your personal and professional life will benefit. True success professionally is how much your personal life is benefited. We work to live, not live to work. That's why your career should work for you and not the other way around. Nailing a positive mindset, building healthy habits, and being able to create your dream work and personal life is what you'll get immediately. And that's just the beginning!

Later in this book, I'll give you nine industry secrets that show you how to dive into and grab IT opportunities with both hands. These chapters are filled with information that will change your life and show you what's possible. But you're first going to learn to appreciate the power of being thankful. Being grateful for where you are and what's to come is the fuel you need for this ride. Buckle up, because with gratitude and determination, you're going places!

MY STORY

In the fall of 1978, I was born to a single mother on Jindo Island, South Korea. My biological father went into the Korean Army since it's mandatory to join and serve for two years. But when he left, she was stuck on an island with no electricity or real opportunity. When she saw little kids running around naked and playing in the dirt, she couldn't imagine raising me there. So, she decided to go back to Seoul. While only she knows the whole story, she didn't tell anyone she was leaving—she grabbed me, caught the ferry, and got out of there as soon as she could.

She went to work at her mother's restaurant, raising me alongside her family. After working at the restaurant for two years, she met a man who came regularly to my grandmother's restaurant. One day, someone was swinging me around in a circle. As fate would have it, my shoulder dislocated and my soon-to-be American dad, who was a medic in the U.S. Army, popped my arm back in its socket. Naturally, he became an instant hero to my grandmother and my mom. Next thing you know, within a year, he and my mom got married. Because of that, I was able to come to the states at just three years old.

We briefly lived in New Jersey, and I got naturalized as an American citizen. We stayed for just one year and then my dad was stationed back in South Korea. Just like that, I ended up back where I was from, but now as an American citizen! This allowed me to go through Department of Defense schools up to fifth grade on the Army post. Then, for the sixth through eighth grades, I entered a Christian school. I wasn't the most well-behaved young man, and I got expelled after just one month of high school. While I don't recommend the same for most people, I never finished high school. Naturally, it didn't take long for me to get into some really bad crowds, going so far as to get initiated into a gang.

Then, when I was 16, I discovered music and became completely fascinated. I was quickly brought into the nightclub scene, and it didn't take me long to meet my first mentor, a famous disc jockey (DJ) in Seoul. I would hang out with him and go to all his clubs and see him spin. He got me an audition at a club called Hackers (there's some foreshadowing at its finest) when I was just 16 years old. That world became my life.

I got into the K-pop scene, rapped for a rock band, did a tour at 17 years old for six months, and then landed my own music deal! It was a wild few years. I was on TV shows and really started to make a name for myself.

However, after we created a full album along with a female vocalist, our manager scammed us and sold our songs to a more famous K-pop band. I was devastated. But even after that, I so badly wanted to be a world-famous DJ; that was still my dream because up until then, I hadn't found anything more promising.

My first huge identity shift in life was going from wanting to be a gangster to discovering music. Music got me out of those environments and into something I was passionate about. But after that didn't work out, I was about to be 18 years old. Therefore, I had to get a job on the military base to get a visa and stay in the country. I worked all kinds of odd jobs at a hotel, from bagging groceries to bussing tables, being a door attendant, and maintenance clerk—you name it. Holding on to my first big dream, I was still doing music on the side.

At that time, my home was a 120-square-foot room in the mountains of Seoul. I was making the equivalent of $5.45 per hour, and in 1999, I made just $6,000 for the entire year. Right after my 19th birthday, my girlfriend and I got married. Within months, I got the news that she was pregnant—a moment that shocked some sense into me because I had no idea how I was going to take care of our baby.

At this stage of my life, the values I had already established, like loyalty, the ability to dream big, and, most importantly, to believe in my dreams, made all the difference. Also, being a provider and a protector was what I knew I just had to do. However, I had no money or promising opportunities. My parents recommended that I go to college or join the military. My first thought was, "Oh, no, that's the last thing I want to do!" But thinking about our newborn baby coming into this world, I had to do something big, especially since I didn't know if my visa was going to be extended otherwise. Going the artistic and musical path started to seem like a less promising option, especially after getting scammed. Worries started to creep in, and I had to do something quickly.

My dad recommended choosing the U.S. Air Force because, at that time, they were as high tech as it got. You have to understand, this was before the dotcom boom. Companies like Yahoo! and MSN and the Internet itself were just coming fully mainstream. Plus, everyone thought the world was going to end in 2000 with the Y2K bug, and the *Matrix* movie just came out. These were some epic times to say the least, where technology was beginning to break through.

Watching the first *Matrix* movie and seeing the IT professionals in the management information systems (MIS) department at my hotel is what ignited my enthusiasm for technology. The behind-the-scenes world of blinking lights and tinted windows made me wildly curious. After getting a job as a maintenance clerk, I bought and got my hands on my first PC. The wealth of information on the Internet was mind-blowing, and I found myself on Yahoo!, searching how to become a "hacker" (remember that first club I auditioned in?).

Experimenting with my PC, I frequently crashed it from tinkering at the kernel level and deep within the operating system. I did a deep-dive into technology, completely geeking out because I knew this was the future. This was one of my life's biggest awakening moments. I couldn't stop dreaming about the possibilities, and providing for my family became my motivation — my "why." I discovered my new passion, and my dream once again shifted. My ambition took off, and I wanted nothing less than to be the best of the best.

So, in 1999, I joined the Air Force to work with technology, and everything fell into place. After basic training, I went to my technical training and got cleared for a Top Secret clearance. At that time, Cisco Systems was building the plumbing of the Internet, and I knew that was where I wanted to eventually work. That became my goal after finishing my Air Force contract.

But while I was still enlisted, after three years working in an IT position, I applied for instructor duty at Keesler Air Force Base in Biloxi, Mississippi. That's where I found I had a passion for teaching. That's also where I learned to teach people in four months what most people waste four years trying to learn. That experience has dictated my life's work because hands-on training is still the best way to gain the real-world skills that you need.

Fast-forward a few years, and I got discharged at 26 years old. I could have immediately transitioned into a role as a network engineer or cyber-security professional for Cisco, but my entrepreneurial spirit had other ideas. So, two of my friends and I became partners, took out a Small Business Administration loan, and started a business with the intention of franchising it. We opened an Internet cafe equipped with 28 PCs that we had custom-built ourselves. We also troubleshooted PCs, hacked Xboxes, and fixed PlayStations. Our cafe was always crowded with people waiting in the lounge for their turn.

On Fridays and Saturdays, we would stay open until 7 a.m. the next day hosting local area network (LAN) parties. (A *LAN party* is where people bring their computers or gaming consoles to one place, connect them through a LAN, and play multiplayer video games together. Since all the devices are connected locally, the games run smoothly with little to no lag. Think of it as a gaming marathon with friends, where you can compete, team up, and enjoy games side by side.) It was an amazing time of life. We were making about $40,000 a month in 2005, and business was booming. And then, Hurricane Katrina hit. It left us devastated and unable to recover. Buried in massive debt from credit cards and loans, I found myself in a deep depression. As the sole breadwinner for a family of four, two of which were my two-year-old and five-year-old daughters, I was constantly wondering where my next paycheck would come from. It felt like my back was against the wall.

But then, I thought, why not return to my original dream? Instead of wanting to be an entrepreneur and franchising Internet cafes across the United States, I decided to go back to the drawing board. Hurricane Katrina served as a reset button for me, which was yet another one of my life-changing aha! moments. People make drastic changes, experience identity shifts, or elevate their lives when their back is against the wall, when they lose everything, or when they are inspired.

Originally, I was inspired to start my career in IT because I saw it was the future. And now, I remembered my dream of working for Cisco Systems. Each time I had an identity shift, it was because I dared to dream of something new. But as a kid, I just wanted to stay in South Korea. I never thought about going to the States until I learned I was going to be a father. That alone made me grow up, take ownership of my life, accept responsibility to raise my family with a secure job that had good medical benefits, and have a sense of peace and security.

That's why Hurricane Katrina was my life's next huge reset. After we closed the Internet cafe, I had to get a job. It all boiled back down to the skills that I learned in the military, including my Top Secret clearance. After a stint at a credit union, a job I was overqualified for, I decided I wanted to go work for Cisco and to become the best engineer I possibly could. Within two years, I went from being in debt and depressed, making only $28,000 at the credit union, to making six figures and then breaking six figures in just 23 months.

After being in the corporate arena for over five years, I asked myself daily, "Is this it? Is this all there is to life?" People asked me how they could become an engineer like me because they knew I didn't have a high school diploma, nor did I go to college to break into that high of a career. Most of the people asking me were going to different universities and college programs, charging anywhere from $40,000 to $120,000 a year for their four-year degree. Sure, you can get the degree—but you don't need that. You need skills, and you need hands-on training in order to be a high-value, highly paid engineer.

I'm an engineer at heart, with an insatiable love for technology. Therefore, at 33 years old, I channeled my passion into the creation of a software project management app for IT teams called Check Action. I poured my life savings and even drained my Cisco 401K, investing around a quarter million dollars into it. Despite the unfortunate crash and burn of the business after 18 months, I was still able to fall back on my core IT skills.

I transitioned from earning $175,000 at Cisco to landing an opportunity at an innovative company, Arista Networks, that was revolutionizing data centers worldwide. The skills I had honed as an engineer and an architect paid off as they secured me a $350,000 compensation package.

At 35 years old, I found myself at the peak of my career, devising seven- to eight-figure IT solutions and crafting IoT solutions for Fortune 500 companies. Repeatedly, CEOs and VPs would express to me how hard it was to find skilled engineers. There was a clear shortage of practical, hands-on training in the industry, with many graduates having useless degrees and overexaggerated résumés.

In 2015, ITT Tech, a once-popular tech training institution, was forced to close for failing to deliver on their promises to students. Hearing the needs of the industry's top leaders and seeing how people were being scammed by colleges, I had an epiphany. I came up with the Zero to Engineer concept, dreaming of creating a platform to provide the essential training and skills CEOs and VPs were desperately seeking in engineers.

Launching a Udemy course (www.udemy.com/course/cisco-engineer-ccna-course-blueprint-101) on how to become a Cisco engineer and earn a six-figure salary marked the beginning of fulfilling my life's greatest dream. As hundreds of students started taking the course, I was reminded of my love for mentoring and teaching. My time as an Air Force instructor was proving to be exactly what I needed to now execute and focus on manifesting my dream into reality.

The fact that so many people got so much from my Udemy course was validation enough, and together with my then cofounder, Jacob, we decided to impact more lives. Jacob was younger but had 15 years of IT experience. We combined our skills and vowed to change the world, giving people practical engineering skills in just four months, in contrast to four years of traditional college. Our vision led to the birth of NGT Academy in 2017. We applied to AngelPad, a top startup incubator, and received our first investment of $50,000. Since then, we've grown to be a multimillion-dollar company.

My journey has been an ever-expanding dream, once hoping to make just $16,000 a year and thinking that $100,000 equaled lifelong wealth. When NGT Academy was launched, the goal was clear. Seven years on, that vision is becoming a reality. I've raised over $18 million, transformed thousands of lives, and remain committed to mentoring one million engineers by 2030.

As billions of devices connect to the IT ecosystem, we are living in amazing times. I hope my story motivates you to dream bigger, believe in yourself, and pursue your goals. It's so important to surround yourself with mentors and supportive people, continuously striving to become an improved version of yourself. Continue reading, and I promise to give you everything needed to go from Zero to Engineer, just like I did.

All in all, I was able to get into my dream job within a decade of coming to the United States. From the first time I dared to dream, I accomplished everything in just 10 years! I believe to master any field you need 10 years, or one decade, to achieve mastery. Made popular by Malcolm Gladwell's book, *Outliers: The Story of Success*, his principle states that in order to become world-class in any field, you need 10,000 hours of deliberate practice. This means 417 days' worth of hours, or 3 hours a day for 3,333 days—this equals a little over 9 years.

But none of that would have been possible had I ever stopped dreaming, lost belief in my dreams, or failed to execute one day at a time. I truly started from zero. When I started to dream of a career in IT, I was bagging groceries and taking inventory of light bulbs with an archaic version of Windows—but for me, that was all I needed.

Had I gotten bogged down in feelings of hopelessness or felt that my dreams were too ambitious, who knows what opportunities would have passed right by me. If you keep your head down, you're likely to miss the signs right in front of you that are pointing you to your best life possible.

Everything could be stripped away, or if you're like me, you could be starting this journey at zero—no certificates, no degree, no experience. But just a dream and a single spark of gratitude is all you need. Combine that with unwavering belief, the ability to execute, and, most importantly, focus, and you're guaranteed to become the hero of your own story, just like me.

And now, it's time to go from Zero to Hero—let's dive in!

CHAPTER SUMMARY, EXERCISES, AND CONCLUSION

Summary

The Power of Dreams

Dreams are the seeds of innovation and progress. They give us a vision of what our future can be and motivate us to work toward it. In the IT field, dreaming big means envisioning yourself in roles that challenge you, inspire you, and allow you to make a significant impact.

- **Dream Big:** Start by allowing yourself to dream without limitations. Picture yourself in your ideal IT career. What are you doing? Who are you working with? What kind of projects are you leading? Write down this vision in as much detail as possible.
- **Set Clear Goals:** Break down your dream into specific, actionable goals. Having a clear road map helps turn your dreams into achievable targets. Identify the skills you need, the certifications required, and the steps necessary to reach your ultimate career goals.

Cultivating Unwavering Belief

Believing in yourself is the cornerstone of success. It's what keeps you going when the path gets tough and what pushes you to overcome obstacles.

- **Self-Confidence:** Confidence is built through small, consistent successes. Celebrate your achievements, no matter how minor they may seem. Each step forward is a testament to your capabilities.
- **Positive Affirmations:** Regularly remind yourself of your strengths and past successes. Positive affirmations can rewire your brain to focus on your abilities rather than your limitations.

- **Resilience:** Embrace failures and setbacks as learning opportunities. Each challenge you overcome strengthens your resilience and brings you closer to your goals.

Exercises

These exercises are designed to help you explore your dreams, build belief, and set a solid foundation for your IT career journey.

Dream Journal Exercise

Objective: To clearly define your career dreams and goals.
Instructions:

- Take 15–20 minutes to write down your biggest career dreams and goals in detail. Be specific about the role you want to achieve, the kind of projects you want to work on, and the impact you want to make in the IT field. Revisit this journal weekly to reflect on your progress and make any necessary adjustments to your goals.

Belief Statements Exercise

Objective: To build self-confidence through positive affirmations.
Instructions:

- Create a list of 10 positive affirmations that reinforce your belief in your ability to achieve your dreams. Examples include "I am capable of learning and mastering new skills," "I can overcome any challenge I face," and "I am on the path to a successful IT career." Repeat these affirmations daily, preferably in front of a mirror, to boost your confidence and resilience.

Visualization Exercise

Objective: To strengthen your belief in achieving your career goals through visualization.

Instructions:

- Spend 5–10 minutes each day visualizing yourself achieving your career goals. Find a quiet space, close your eyes, and imagine the steps you'll take, the challenges you'll overcome, and the success you'll achieve. Picture yourself in your dream role, working on exciting projects, and making a significant impact. Feel the emotions associated with these achievements, such as pride, joy, and fulfillment.

By completing these exercises, you'll not only gain clarity on your career dreams and goals but also build the confidence and resilience needed to achieve them. Remember, the journey to success begins with daring to dream and believing in your potential. Start today, and let your dreams guide you to a successful IT career.

Conclusion

Daring to dream and believing in yourself are the first steps toward a successful IT career. With a clear vision, unwavering belief, and a solid action plan, you can achieve anything you set your mind to. Remember, every expert was once a beginner who dared to dream and believed in their potential. Start your journey today, and let your dreams guide you to greatness.

CHAPTER TWO

FROM ZERO TO HERO: THE MINDSET YOU NEED TO SUCCEED IN IT

"Whatever the mind can conceive and believe, it can achieve."
— Napoleon Hill, American author

INTRODUCTION

Before we dive into everything you need to know about the IT ecosystem, let's talk about something important that will guide you through not only this book but also your entire journey in IT—your mindset. Mindset is like the lens through which you see and make sense of the world. There are mainly two types of mindsets: a fixed mindset or a growth one. But let's not just throw around concepts. Let me tell you an incredible story that explains it all.

Picture this: It's the early 1950s, and there's a common belief that no human can run a mile in under 4 minutes. Doctors, athletes, and pretty much everyone else think it's impossible—that our bodies simply are not capable of it. This belief is so strong that it's like a brick wall in people's minds.

Enter Roger Bannister. Roger is a medical student and a runner, but in no way is he superhuman. For years, he hears everyone saying that the 4-minute barrier is unbreakable. But guess what? He doesn't buy it. Instead of thinking, "This is impossible," he thinks, "How can I do this?"

Here's where it gets exciting. Roger doesn't just dream about it; he set his mind to break that barrier. He trained differently, thought differently, and believed differently. He put on his running shoes and set foot on the track with a single goal in his mind: to break the 4-minute mile.

And then, on May 6, 1954, in front of a cheering crowd and against all odds, Roger Bannister did the unthinkable. He ran a mile in 3 minutes and 59.4 seconds! He trusted himself, he made consistent action to achieve success, and most of all, he smashed through that brick wall in people's minds. Whether or not he knew it then, he became a real-life superhero.

After Roger broke this record, something amazing happened. Within just a few years, many other runners started doing what was thought to be impossible. Today, running a mile in under 4 minutes is a basic standard for middle-distance runners.

So, what happened here? Did humans suddenly evolve into a different species? Nope. Roger Bannister changed the mindset and grew the potential of what humans are capable of. His story is the perfect example of what can be achieved with a growth mindset—the belief that with effort, learning, and persistence, there's no limit to what you can achieve.

Now, think about yourself. As you step into the IT world, are you going to let the "brick walls" stop you? Or are you going to be like Roger Bannister and believe in the possibilities? So many people set limiting beliefs that in order to make $100,000+ in this industry, you need a college degree, to have 10 to 20 years of experience, to be an executive, and so on. There are endless excuses you can make—brick walls you can build—that keep you from achieving your goals. Don't forget, with just an eighth grade education and the right training and experience, I broke into the IT ecosystem and made a $350,000 salary.

Your mindset is key for your journey going from Zero to Hero of your own life. In this chapter, we'll delve deeper into the concepts of fixed and growth mindsets, and how a growth mindset will be your secret weapon in the IT world.

Ready to break barriers? Let's get started!

GROWTH vs. FIXED MINDSET

Another great quote by Napoleon Hill is, "Our only limitations are the ones we set up in our own minds." We've all been there, telling ourselves, "I'm not good enough. I don't think I can do this." But to grow, we must learn to recognize that those thoughts are just self-doubt creeping up in our mind.

Having a growth mindset is not about how good you are—it's about how great you want to be. Think about that for a moment. That means you must believe in what's possible first *before* you can shift your mindset.

Succeeding is not only about what you can do right now, but about what you want to be able to do. To have a growth mindset, you need to believe that you can do more. When you change how you think, new opportunities will inevitably show up in your life.

Now, let's talk about the opposite, which is having a fixed mindset. This way of living has huge drawbacks that will hold back your personal and professional development.

A person with a fixed mindset often believes that talents and skills are something other people are just born with. They look at successful people, like professional baseball players, and assume they were simply born gifted, saying their success is from their DNA rather than effort. But we know that's complete BS!

Achieving success in any field involves discipline, repetition, and a considerable amount of hard work. That's why having a fixed mindset limits your capacity for growth and improvement, which will lead to stagnation and tons of missed opportunities.

Having a fixed mindset causes people to avoid challenges out of fear. So many people fear that failure will reveal a lack of skill. But that's not how life works. Failure is needed to learn! Having a fixed mindset blocks you from not only appreciating when you win but from seeing the huge value that comes from failure. Also, it will cause you to give up easily when faced with obstacles, believing you simply don't possess the ability to overcome them.

This is particularly detrimental in the IT field, which constantly evolves and presents new challenges. For instance, while working on a new project, you will inevitably encounter a complex technical issue. A fixed mindset might see this as an insurmountable hurdle or an exhausting problem, whereas a growth mindset would view it as an opportunity to learn, grow, and develop new skills.

The road to success is littered with obstacles and challenges. It is your mindset that determines whether these obstacles become roadblocks or stepping stones. Think of it like a spiral; your mindset shapes how you tackle challenges and deal with life. The growth mindset keeps spiraling up, as you keep getting better. But with a fixed mindset, you might spiral down and get stuck. That's why avoiding a fixed mindset is crucial for personal growth and career advancement.

There are a few signs that show us if someone thinks they can or cannot grow. Let's look at what these signs are:

1. Facing Challenges:
   - Fixed Mindset: Says "This is too hard, I'd rather not."
   - Growth Mindset: Says "This is new and exciting. Let's try it!"

2. Dealing with Obstacles:
   - Fixed Mindset: Scared and doubtful.
   - Growth Mindset: Optimistic and ready to tackle them.
3. Effort:
   - Fixed Mindset: Wants easy wins, doesn't work hard.
   - Growth Mindset: Puts in the work to get results.
4. Handling Criticism:
   - Fixed Mindset: Gets upset and sees it as an attack.
   - Growth Mindset: Sees it as a way to improve.
5. Seeing Others Succeed:
   - Fixed Mindset: Gets jealous and makes excuses for others' success.
   - Growth Mindset: Gets inspired and motivated by others' success.

Facing Challenges

When observing someone with a fixed mindset faces challenges, you'll often find that they approach these challenges with doubt, reluctance, or frustration. They might think, "This seems too hard," or "I'd rather not do it." They aren't excited about the challenge and might even try to avoid it.

On the other hand, someone with a growth mindset is much more likely to embrace challenges with enthusiasm. For example, take yourself reading this very book, eager and ready to dive into possibilities. Even though what you learn may be new and push you into places you've never been, you're embracing it with an open mind. That's a key characteristic of a growth mindset!

Dealing with Obstacles

Now, let's talk about facing obstacles. For someone with a fixed mindset, the initial reactions are often doubt and fear. They might see an obstacle as a sign that they're not cut out for the task at hand.

Contrast this with how a person with a growth mindset views obstacles. They are likely to be more open and optimistic. They see an obstacle not as a dead end, but as just another part of the journey that they are excited to navigate through.

This difference in attitudes toward challenges and obstacles is fundamental. Embracing challenges and viewing obstacles as opportunities for growth is super empowering and will contribute to greater success and fulfillment.

Effort

When we consider effort, what do you think a person with a fixed mindset imagines? In their head, it's all about minimal effort—doing the bare minimum. They often wish everything would just be spoon-fed to them, don't they?

On the flip side, how does someone with a growth mindset approach effort? They are proactive and have a "do whatever it takes" mentality. For individuals with a growth mindset, effort is synonymous with the hard work they are willing to put in. They don't shy away from rolling up their sleeves and getting their hands dirty because they understand that putting in that extra effort is what leads to real results. This also means making self-care and a positive mental attitude their main priority. Sometimes it takes effort to work out, meditate, or go for a walk, but it's always worth it.

This difference in attitudes toward effort is a game changer. A fixed mindset leads to seeking shortcuts and avoiding hard work, whereas a growth mindset is all about embracing the whole journey, knowing that it's an essential part of progress and success. It's vital to recognize this contrast, as it can be a determining factor in achieving your goals and aspirations.

Handling Criticism

Picture this: Someone with a fixed mindset is given words of constructive criticism. They're likely to react quite defensively, like, "Whoa, why is this person telling me this?" They usually have a negative vibe about it, as if they're thinking, "Oh great, this person thinks they can school me on this." They're closed off, like they don't need anybody's two cents. Or when someone is rude to a person with a fixed mindset, they take the rudeness personally instead of realizing someone being rude is their own issue.

And here's why that's such a bummer when you're looking to grow. With a fixed mindset, you're shutting the door on folks who are trying to give you pointers that could help patch up your weak spots or learning to be kind to rude people. It's like putting on blinders; you just don't want to see it.

Now, let's switch gears to someone with a growth mindset. They're pretty much the opposite. They actually crave feedback. They're like, "Lay it on me! I want to get better!" They welcome the guidance with open arms because they know it's only going to help their development. It's the secret sauce that can help them step up their game.

So, the takeaway here is pretty clear: Being open to criticism is key for growth. If you've got a fixed mindset, you're putting up barriers. But with a growth mindset, you're tearing those walls down and inviting in the wisdom and insights that can really make a difference. It's like choosing between staying in a cocoon or spreading your wings to fly.

Seeing Others Succeed

All right, now let's explore another area where people get all tangled up. How do people with fixed and growth mindsets perceive the success of others? Well, someone with a fixed mindset tends to get uneasy around the success of others. They might even be scared by it. They think, "That could have been me, but now it's too late."

🔒 FIXED MINDSET	📊 GROWTH MINDSET
▸ Success comes from talent.	▸ Success comes from effort.
▸ I'm either smart or dumb.	▸ I can grow my intelligence.
▸ I don't like challenges.	▸ I embrace challenges as a chance to grow.
▸ Failure means I can't do it.	▸ Failure means I'm learning.
▸ Feedback is a personal attack.	▸ Feedback is necessary and constructive.
▸ If you succeed, I feel threatened.	▸ If you succeed, I'm inspired.
▸ If something's too hard I give up.	▸ I keep trying even when I'm frustrated.

On the flip side, those with a growth mindset see someone who's thriving and get pumped up by it. Picture this: You're at work, and you see a colleague absolutely nailing a project. If you've got a fixed mindset, that might freak you out. You might start worrying they're gunning for your job or something. You might even start making excuses for their success—"Oh, they were born into money," or "They just got lucky." People with fixed mindsets tend to have negative, judgmental reactions that are extremely limiting.

You might even be able to recall some people you've crossed paths with who fit this mold. They were the ones dismissing others' accomplishments by saying things like, "Well, that person was born with a higher IQ," and so on. It's a strange way to think, but unfortunately, it's quite common. This kind of mindset creates a belief that we're shackled by our circumstances, which is exactly what we're trying to break away from.

Now, contrast that with a growth mindset, where seeing others succeed lights a fire under you. These people become your mentors, your guides on your journey to success. They inspire and motivate you, and most importantly, they provide a learning opportunity. Regardless of your chosen field or ambition—be it a systems engineer, architect, CEO, or anything else—seek out someone who's already there. Learn from them. Be humble and open-minded. Doing so will change your world.

> *"When old patterns are broken, new worlds emerge."*
> —*Tuli Kupferberg*

The key here is to shift from a fixed mindset, which is constrictive and limiting, to a growth mindset, which is expansive and liberating. The success of others is not a threat; it's an opportunity. Be inspired, be motivated, and above all, be ready to learn and grow.

LIVING, WORKING, AND BREATHING A GROWTH MINDSET

So now that you're getting the hang of developing a growth mindset, it's time to grasp just how much untapped potential you have. Seriously, you're like a treasure chest waiting to be opened. But let's be real, we're not all at our peak, right? We all can do better and climb higher.

So, what's the game plan? It's simple: Take action. Think of Roger Bannister. He had a dream, a wild goal. Most of all, he knew he had the potential. So, what did he do? He hustled! He put his heart and soul into training every day until he removed that 4-minute barrier.

And here's the magic—doing something like this rebuilds your belief system. You start thinking, "Hey, I can actually do this!" Confidence goes up, you understand yourself better, and guess what? You start seeing even more potential in yourself. It's like leveling up in a video game.

Now, here's the thing—you gotta make sure your actions and the advice you follow is on point. You don't take karate lessons from someone who's only watched action movies, right? So, whatever your dream is—let's say becoming a network architect at Coca-Cola or landing a gig at Cisco—follow someone who's been there and done that.

Here's where it gets crucial. You have to go all in! Some people might try a little bit and then back off. Why? Because they don't want to give it their all. They're thinking they can just breeze through with minimal effort. But if you've got a growth mindset, you're looking at this mountain of effort and thinking, "I've got my climbing gear ready!"

But let's not forget—your actions need to be in tune with the situation. The world's always changing—you've got to adapt and make the right moves at the right time.

Imagine it like that spiral I mentioned; you always want to be on the upward spiral. This isn't just about moving in circles; it's about climbing to new heights. Yeah, it can go the other way too, but we're here for the upward climb!

So, in a nutshell, it's like this: Tap into your potential, take focused and massive action, and start getting the results. Each victory, big or small, will build that confidence and belief system. Keep that spiral going up!

CLEAR MIND, CONFIDENT LIFE

Having a clear vision is fundamental to personal or professional success, and it starts with creating the right mindset. By choosing to read this book, you've already set an objective for yourself as you go from Zero to Engineer. Maybe a coworker or family member recommended it to you, or you had a personal realization that you need to take immediate action to begin a rock-solid career. Whatever the reason, with what I share with you in this book, you will be able to visualize your future as an engineer or specialist in the IT industry.

This initial thought blossoms into a vision, which becomes increasingly clear as you build confidence toward it. Throughout this book and your professional life, the rule of Kaizen—meaning "change for good" or "continuous improvement" in Japanese—should guide you. This concept is so important to me that it's tattooed on my arm! Kaizen can be applied to both personal and professional life, and I encourage you to utilize it throughout your career.

Remember, progress is about taking one step at a time. Instead of fixating on the end goal, cherish the journey. A powerful quote of **Lao Tzu** encapsulates this perfectly: "Watch your thoughts, for they become words. Watch your words, for they become actions. Watch your actions, for they become habits. Watch your habits, for they become character. Watch your character, for it becomes your destiny."

Success starts with a thought, an idea, a clear vision. Observing your thoughts is an enlightening exercise. Researchers Julie Tseng and Jordan Poppenk suggest we have 6,000 thoughts per day (www.queensu.ca/gazette/stories/discovery-thought-worms-opens-window-mind). That's astonishing, isn't it? It's crucial to realize that not all these thoughts originate from you. We consume massive amounts of information daily—through social media, news, and conversations. But mastering your mind and thoughts is possible. Channel your energy into positive thinking, then take action on those thoughts, ideas, or visions. These actions will become habits, and in turn, define your identity. This identity, which is your character, shapes your destiny.

Achieving success requires hard work and tenacity. It's all too common for people to back down in the face of challenges. But creating a growth mindset fuels your resilience to overcome setbacks because they are merely learning opportunities. Rejection is a part of the process. You may not land every job you interview for, but the key is not to give up. Also, the willingness to make sacrifices and commit to a goal is paramount.

Creating an environment of discipline is equally crucial. Show up, take consistent action, be accountable, and take yourself seriously. Recognize failures as stepping stones to learning. Remember, persistence is key to overcoming obstacles. There may be risks associated with success, but people only see the tip of the iceberg, not what's beneath. It's the journey, with all its challenges and triumphs, that truly counts. Over time, you may even come to enjoy this process because it fosters growth, builds your confidence, and helps you level up, which is our ultimate goal at NGT Academy.

CHAPTER SUMMARY, EXERCISES, ACTION PLAN, AND CONCLUSION

Summary

Achieving success in the dynamic world of information technology requires more than just technical proficiency. It demands a robust mindset characterized by resilience, adaptability, and a perpetual eagerness to learn. This chapter delved into the essential mental attitudes needed to excel from an entry-level position to a distinguished IT professional.

Embracing the Growth Mindset

The concept of the growth mindset, introduced by psychologist Carol Dweck, is foundational in the IT industry. It's the belief that intelligence and abilities can develop over time through effort, good teaching, and persistence.

Challenges as Opportunities

Recognize challenges as valuable learning experiences that drive growth. This mindset will empower you to overcome obstacles and continuously improve throughout your career journey.

- **View Every Challenge as an Opportunity to Grow:** Whether it's a difficult project or learning a new technology, see these situations as chances to enhance your skills.
- **Persistence Against Setbacks:** In IT, setbacks are not just possible but expected. Learning from mistakes and persevering sets the groundwork for future successes.
- **Feedback for Growth:** Actively seek out feedback and use it constructively. Embrace both positive and negative feedback as valuable information to guide your learning and career development.

Building Resilience

Resilience is your emotional strength to bounce back from adversity. It's crucial for dealing with the fast pace and frequent changes inherent in the tech world.

- **Develop Coping Mechanisms:** Identify personal strategies that help you manage stress effectively. This could be regular exercise, hobbies, or meditation.
- **Adaptability:** Stay flexible and open to change. The tech landscape is continuously evolving, and adaptability is key to staying relevant.
- **Realistic Goal Setting:** Set achievable goals that motivate you without setting you up for failure. Break larger objectives into smaller, manageable tasks that provide regular satisfaction and progress.

Cultivating Continuous Learning

The only constant in technology is change. Staying updated with the latest developments is not just beneficial; it's essential.

- **Lifelong Learning Commitment:** Make a commitment to ongoing learning. This can involve taking courses, attending workshops, or participating in webinars.
- **Leverage Resources:** Use online platforms like Coursera, LinkedIn Learning, and industry certifications to keep your skills sharp and current.
- **Learn from Peers:** Engage with your community, join forums, attend tech meetups, and learn from the experiences and knowledge of your peers.

Fostering Positive Thinking

A positive outlook can dramatically influence your career trajectory. It enhances your ability to cope with challenges and influences your willingness to take on new opportunities.

- **Practice Gratitude:** Regularly reflect on and appreciate your achievements and the opportunities you have been given. This can help you maintain a positive and motivated mindset.
- **Visualize Success:** Regular visualization of achieving your goals can reinforce your career aspirations and boost your confidence to achieve them.
- **Positive Environment:** Surround yourself with supportive colleagues and mentors. Their encouragement and insight can be vital during challenging times.

Exercises

Fixed vs. Growth Mindset Reflection

Objective: Identify areas where you currently have a fixed mindset and actively shift toward a growth mindset.

Instructions:

- Make two columns in a journal: "Fixed Mindset" and "Growth Mindset."
- Reflect on situations where you've said things like "I can't do this" or "I'm just not good at it." Write those thoughts under the "Fixed Mindset" column.
- In the "Growth Mindset" column, reframe those statements. For example, "I'm not good at this" becomes "I'm learning how to do this better."
- Review this list weekly to track progress in adopting a growth mindset in specific areas.

Growth Challenges Tracker

Objective: Develop a habit of embracing challenges as learning opportunities.
Instructions:

- Choose one task or skill each week that you find challenging (e.g., learning a new technology, speaking up in meetings).
- Track your thoughts and emotions before, during, and after engaging with the challenge. Reflect on what you learned from the experience, even if you didn't succeed immediately.
- Write down the next small step you'll take toward mastery of that skill or task. Repeat this weekly to build momentum and confidence.

Daily Gratitude Practice

Objective: Cultivate a growth-oriented mindset by recognizing the positives in your life and reframing challenges as opportunities for growth.

Instructions:

1. **Morning and Evening Reflection:**
   - **Morning:**
     - Start your day by listing **three things you are grateful for**. These can be related to personal life, career, or learning opportunities. Examples include:
       - "I'm grateful for access to IT training resources."
       - "I'm thankful for the opportunity to improve my networking skills today."
       - "I'm grateful for a fresh start to make progress toward my goals."
   - **Evening:**
     - At the end of the day, reflect on **three positive moments or accomplishments**. This could be something like:
       - "I solved a tricky troubleshooting issue."
       - "I had a great conversation with a mentor."
       - "I completed a chapter in my certification course."

2. **Challenge Reflection:**
   - Identify **one challenge you faced** during the day and reframe it as an opportunity.
     - Example: "Today's networking problem taught me how to remain calm under pressure."
     - Write: "Because of this experience, I am better prepared to handle similar situations in the future."

Kaizen Stepping Stones

Objective: Apply the principles of **Kaizen**—continuous, incremental improvement—to build a growth mindset and achieve long-term goals by breaking them into small, manageable steps.

Instructions:

1. **Define a Long-Term Goal:**
   - Write down one meaningful career or personal development goal.
     - Example: "Become a certified cloud engineer within one year."

2. **Identify Stepping Stones (Small Wins):**
   - Break the long-term goal into **5–7 small, actionable tasks**. These should be achievable in short timeframes (1–3 days).
     - Example:
       - Research certification programs today.
       - Enroll in a cloud engineering course.
       - Spend 30 minutes each day learning a new concept.
       - Practice hands-on labs twice a week.
       - Join a study group or online forum.

3. **Daily Kaizen Reflection:**
   - At the end of each day, reflect on **one small action** you completed toward your goal.
     - Example: "Today, I explored AWS Labs for 30 minutes."
   - Ask: "What worked well? What could be improved tomorrow?"

4. **Progress Tracker:**
   - Create a **visual progress tracker**—it could be a list, a Kanban board, or a stepping stone graphic. Check off each small task as you complete it. This reinforces progress and builds momentum.

5. **Celebrate Small Wins:**
   - For every few tasks completed, reward yourself with **small celebrations** to acknowledge progress.
     - Example: After completing the first 5 tasks, take a break or treat yourself to a coffee.

6. **Adjust Your Path Weekly:**
   - At the end of the week, review your progress. If any task feels too big, **break it down further** into even smaller steps. This reflects the Kaizen mindset—improvement through tiny, continuous actions.

This exercise helps you build momentum by focusing on **small daily actions**. Over time, these micro-efforts accumulate into significant progress, shifting your mindset toward continuous learning and improvement. It embodies the Kaizen philosophy—achieving excellence one step at a time.

Conclusion

Here are the primary tools necessary for fostering the right mindset:

- **Positive Thinking:** It's crucial to maintain a positive frame of mind as your thoughts influence your reality. Stay away from negativity and focus on positive aspects.
- **Focus on the Big Picture:** Keep your long-term goals in perspective. Be patient and recognize that significant achievements take time. Think about where you want to be years down the line. As Bill Gates wisely said, "People overestimate what they can accomplish in one year and underestimate what they can accomplish in a decade."
- **Practice Gratitude:** Integrating gratitude into your daily routine has proven benefits like reduced stress and increased happiness. This positive attitude can fuel your productivity.
- **Embrace the Journey:** Take pride and find joy in the path you are on. Acknowledge that the process of learning and growing is an adventure and embrace it fully.

Having equipped yourself with these tools, it's important to understand that they're not stand-alone. They interact and reinforce each other in building a robust mindset. A growth mindset is not just about positive thinking; it's also about understanding the broader picture, being thankful for what you have, and taking pleasure in the process. This mindset will form the bedrock on which you can build habits that are conducive to your growth.

In the next chapter, we will look at how you can incorporate these tools in everyday life and build habits that sustain a growth mindset. We'll explore how this is just the beginning of laying a foundation that supports your personal life as well as your career as an IT professional. So, continue to the next chapter with an open mind, ready to learn and grow!

CHAPTER THREE

HABITS AND RITUALS

"Both success and failure are largely the results of habit."
— Napoleon Hill

INTRODUCTION

In this chapter, I will guide you through something that will determine the sustainability of your success—habits. You might think you know what's up with habits, but there's way more than meets the eye. Don't believe me? Take a moment to reflect, on the choices you make, the things you do every day—it's all habits. The way you brush your teeth, how you walk to your car, what you listen to in the car, the thoughts you have when you start to get tired, the kind of food you eat . . . it's all habits.

I'm going to walk you through how you can shape your life by up-leveling your habits. I'll share with you my strategy, and that means having a system. We'll start by focusing on the power of the morning routine. You'll see how the early hours of the day, when everything is fresh, is the launchpad for an amazing day.

I'll also show you how I use meditation to keep my mind sharp and clear. And no, it's not just for monks on a mountain. Meditation is a highly practical tool—and a powerful one at that. You'll learn how to use it to create the life you've always wanted. And let's not forget the importance of being thankful. Gratitude is what makes it all work, and worth it.

We'll also explore how your body plays a huge part in all of this. Stretching, staying hydrated—it all adds up. And I'll show you how planning and scheduling isn't just something boring. It's like making your very own treasure map to success. Just when you think you've got everything you need, I'm going to introduce you to a couple of books that are game changers.

KAIZEN

IMPROVEMENT QUALITY ADVANCEMENT CONTINUOUS SUCCESS IMPLEMENTATION

YOU MUST HAVE A RISING RITUAL

I cannot emphasize enough how your morning is the launchpad for your day. It's like priming a rocket for take-off—the energy and vibe you set in the morning dictates how the rest of the day unfolds. While there's nothing wrong with having off days, you need to have the tools at your disposal so your life isn't determined by your good days or your bad days. To become the true creator of your own life, you have to have rituals and systems that you build around you that keep you growing.

I'll give you a glimpse into my mornings. This routine has been an absolute game changer for me. As soon as I realize that I'm awake, and before I even open my eyes, that's when the magic starts. My brain is still coasting on calm theta waves, and this is the perfect time to feel deep gratitude. However, if I feel like I'll fall back asleep, I'll stand up, especially if I'm procrastinating and wanting to hit snooze. Getting your body moving and your blood pumping is a way better start to your day than falling into old habits and mindlessly scrolling through your phone on Instagram or Facebook. Trust me, picking up your phone should be the last thing you want to do first thing in the morning.

But as best you can, before you look at anything or take in the room or world around you, practice gratitude. It's like opening the windows of your soul and letting the sunshine in. Speaking of sunshine, I always aim to rise with the sun. This helps your body align with the circadian rhythm so that you can have a deep rest, along with many more benefits.

Then what I do is think about three things I'm grateful for. Simple. It could be anything—the fact that I had a peaceful sleep, my family, or even for my trusty bottle of water that awaits me.

Speaking of water, you want to drink water soon after waking up, right after your gratitude practice and brushing your teeth. And not just a sip—I go for a full 16 to 24 ounces. It gives your body a much-needed rejuvenation. It flushes out toxins and gears you up for the day. Squeeze a lemon into your water; your immune system will thank you, and you'll kick-start your metabolism.

Now back to gratitude and meditation. After listing those three things, brushing your teeth, and drinking water, take a few minutes to drop into a meditation. You can even do just 2 minutes. And no, meditation isn't just for monks. It's a powerful tool that you can wield to craft a better reality for yourself.

I like to begin my meditation with visualization. Close your eyes and imagine—really imagine—where you want to be. See yourself crossing the finish line of a certification program with your friends and family beaming at you. Picture yourself walking into your dream job and feel the handshake as they welcome you aboard. Imagine the joy of achieving your goals, whether it's a promotion, a vacation, or a new car.

But here's the most important part: You've got to *feel* it. Don't just see it; let it tug at your heartstrings. Emotions are what tie your dreams to your real life. They are what tells the universe that you are serious about what you want. Dedicate at least 10 minutes of your morning to this, and you'll be surprised how quickly the pieces start falling into place.

Next up is stretching and moving. You've got to get your body out of its slumber. Stretch, use a foam roller, grab the jump rope again, and feel your muscles wake up. The morning is a great time to work out—but no matter what, some form of moving around is essential. It's about telling your body that it's a new day, and you're ready to get going. Also, as soon as possible, get outside and in direct sunlight, and be sure to do this whole routine without looking at your phone, without exception.

KEEP UP THE MOMENTUM

Succeeding in your personal and professional life requires a lot more than a consistent and effective morning ritual. You've got to be able to keep the momentum going through every part of your day. If you want to achieve your goals, you have to be intentional and present to all aspects of your life. The path from Zero to Engineer and being a six-figure earner demands it.

To keep it simple, I'll show you how to optimize your day with good habits. By breaking my day into these segments, I stay on track and can focus on fully owning that part of my day. And if I miss any of the practices in that time chunk, instead of letting it ruin my whole day I simply focus on owning the next chunk of time. This keeps me fully accountable and guilt-free, which I've found is the balance necessary to make real, lasting change in life.

That's what you're here for, right? To fully show up and take complete ownership of your life? You've already made a significant investment in yourself by buying this book. So, let's do it! Here are the five segments of an optimized day:

1. Rise and Shine
2. Midday Money-Makers
3. Afternoon Action
4. Evening Enjoyment
5. Nighttime Necessities

Rise and Shine

As I already broke down for you, the morning is a pivotal time to set the tone for the day. But here are some more tips to have a powerful morning. If you choose to work out in the morning, end it with a cold shower! Cold showers improve circulation, boost your mood, and sharpen mental clarity. And what is the natural thing to do when you get in freezing cold water? To take a huge breath in. So, use the intelligence of your body and include deep breathing or breathwork before, during, and after your cold shower. This will align your mind and body and give you prolonged focus.

What about breakfast? The key idea here is to eat more fatty foods, no sugar, or don't eat at all. Why? Sugars can cause insulin spikes, leading to an energy crash. Go for good fats, such as avocados or nuts, which provide steady energy. Lastly, use essential supplements, such as Omega-3s and Vitamins D and B12. If you want to eat but it's processed, sugary, or greasy food, you're much better off fasting until you eat a rock-solid lunch. This is why I intermittently fast and do a 24-hour fast once a week.

Midday Money-Makers

This segment is all about productivity. If you're commuting, instead of letting stress take the wheel, turn this time into an opportunity for self-reflection and learning. Exchange music for podcasts or audiobooks. Something else that will profoundly help your productivity is to use adaptogens like ashwagandha, lion's mane mushrooms, and many others. They also work in tandem with power plants like cacao, yerba mate, or matcha to improve mental performance. These are excellent alternatives to coffee. Yuck.

Then, after an empowering commute (or if you work from home and it's just walking to your desk), when you get there it's essential to have a tidy workspace. This reflects and promotes a clear mind. Integrate movement and regular breaks into your workday to keep the energy flowing. Also, make sure you protect your focus by setting boundaries with those who could distract you and allocate specific times for deep, uninterrupted work.

Afternoon Action

Lunchtime should be prioritized! Meal-prepping healthy foods is usually the most affordable option. But if you prefer dining out, seek out restaurants that source their ingredients from local farms or at least use organic ingredients. Post-eating, take a binaural nap. Listening to binaural beats for just 15 minutes is proven to improve memory and creativity. This allows you to finish the workday strong and keep up your energy and focus. The late afternoon or after work is another fantastic time to work out if you didn't that morning. You have options: Level 1 is just about light movement like going for a walk or easy hike, Level 2 is a full-body workout (do this at least three times a week), and Level 3 involves specialized training with a professional. And don't forget to finish it off with a cold shower and deep breaths and make them the deepest breaths you take all day.

Evening Enjoyment

As the day winds down, it's essential to shift gears. This is a time to reconnect with yourself and your loved ones. Limit electronic use, meditate again (because why not?), or play an instrument. Spend quality time with your spouse, children, or pets, and do as much of this as you can outdoors. For dinner, focus on nourishment, not how fast you can prepare it. Choose ingredients and recipes that make you feel like you are treating yourself after a day of locked-in habits. The evening is also a great time for journaling or reflection. Consider what went well during the day and what you could improve on.

Nighttime Necessities

Setting the stage for a restful sleep is your number-one priority. Engage in activities that are fulfilling but not overly stimulating such as reading or playing non-video games. It's essential to limit LED blue light exposure and to also create a sleep-conducive environment. Remove any electronics or TVs from the bedroom and make sure you have plants, which purify the air as you sleep. And to close off your day, a nighttime routine that is basically the mirror image of your morning routine will help you keep the good habits going. Drink water, brush your teeth, meditate, and then right as you lay down, begin listing all the things you're grateful for, thinking positive thoughts, doing a visual meditation, and affirmations. What we think about as we fall asleep is what we program into our subconscious mind and what determines much of our success.

CHAPTER SUMMARY, EXERCISES, AND CONCLUSION

Summary

Success in the fast-paced world of information technology is not solely determined by what you know, but also by how you apply your knowledge daily. Establishing productive habits and rituals is crucial for maintaining efficiency, enhancing skill levels, and achieving long-term career goals.

This chapter explores the key habits and daily rituals that can transform your IT career.

Establishing Productive Habits

Productive habits are the building blocks of a successful career. They ensure that you consistently perform at your best and continue to grow professionally.

- **Time Management:** Effective time management allows you to maximize productivity. Prioritize tasks using techniques like the Eisenhower Matrix (https://todoist.com/productivity-methods/eisenhower-matrix) or the Pomodoro Technique (www.pomodorotechnique.com) to manage your day efficiently.
- **Continuous Learning:** Make learning a daily habit. Dedicate time each day or week to update your skills and knowledge. This can include reading articles, taking online courses, or experimenting with new technologies.
- **Networking:** Regular interaction with peers and mentors can provide insights, opportunities, and support. Make it a habit to connect with other professionals in your field through social media, conferences, and local meetups.

Creating Rituals for Success

Rituals are sequences of activities performed in a particular order and at a specific time. They can set the tone for your day, boost your productivity, and help manage stress.

- **Morning Rituals:** Start your day with a routine that prepares you mentally and physically. This might include exercise, meditation, reviewing your goals, or reading industry news.

- **Workday Start-Up Ritual:** Begin your workday with a consistent set of tasks, such as reviewing your to-do list, setting daily objectives, or clearing your workspace. This signals to your brain that it's time to focus.
- **Evening Wind-Down Ritual:** End your day with activities that help you unwind and reflect. This could involve reviewing what you accomplished, planning for the next day, or spending time on a hobby.

The Role of Technology in Habit Formation

Leverage technology to reinforce and track your habits. Various apps and tools can help you manage your time, learn new skills, and connect with others.

- **Time Management Apps:** Use apps like Trello, Asana, or Todoist to keep track of tasks and deadlines. I also love using Trello to set up my digital vision board.
- **Learning Platforms:** Platforms like NGT Academy, YouTube, Udemy, Coursera, or Pluralsight offer courses on a wide range of IT topics. Set reminders to log in and learn.
- **Networking Tools:** LinkedIn and Meetup are excellent for finding and attending industry events or connecting with other professionals.

Habits of Successful IT Professionals

Learn from the best by understanding the habits of successful IT leaders.

- **Discipline:** Successful professionals are disciplined in their approach to work and learning. They set high standards for themselves and consistently meet them.
- **Curiosity:** They maintain an insatiable curiosity about technological advancements and industry trends, always looking for better ways to solve problems.

- **Resilience:** They quickly recover from setbacks and view failures as opportunities to learn and grow.

Exercises

Habit Identification and Awareness Worksheet

Objective: Identify your current habits and assess their impact on your personal and professional life.

Instructions:

1. List **all your daily habits**—from how you start your day to how you wind down at night.
2. Categorize each habit as **productive, neutral, or unproductive**.
   - Productive habits contribute positively toward your goals (e.g., morning exercise).
   - Neutral habits don't help or harm (e.g., scrolling through social media occasionally).
   - Unproductive habits hinder progress (e.g., procrastinating on tasks).
3. Review your list and **identify patterns**—which productive habits can you enhance, and which unproductive habits need to be replaced or modified?

Build a 30-Day Habit Tracker

Objective: Cultivate consistency by tracking a new habit for 30 days.

Instructions:

1. **Select one new habit** to develop (e.g., reading 10 pages daily or practicing coding).
2. Create a **habit tracker** using a calendar, journal, or digital app.
3. Each day you complete the habit, mark it on the tracker. Aim to build a **streak** by completing the habit daily.

4. If you miss a day, **avoid discouragement**. Instead, reflect on why it happened and adjust to stay on track.

5. At the end of the 30 days, evaluate the experience. Ask yourself: **Did I notice progress? How did this habit impact my day-to-day life?**

Remove and Replace a Negative Habit

Objective: Replace one unproductive habit with a positive one to promote growth and success.

Instructions:

1. Identify **one unproductive habit** you want to remove (e.g., scrolling through social media in bed).

2. Select a **productive habit** to replace it with (e.g., reading a book before bed or preparing tomorrow's to-do list).

3. Create a **reminder or trigger** to help you stay on track (e.g., place your book on your pillow to remind you to read before sleep).

4. Track your progress for 30 days. Reflect weekly on how replacing the habit has impacted your day.

Incorporate Technology Exercise

Objective: To explore how technology can enhance your productivity, learning, and professional growth.

Instructions:

1. **Explore Tools:** Identify apps or platforms that align with your goals (e.g., Google Calendar for time management, Coursera for learning, LinkedIn for networking).

2. **Experiment with Integration:** Try using one tool per category (time, learning, networking) for a week. See how it fits into your routine naturally.

3. **Adjust and Reflect:** At the end of the week, reflect on which tools added value. Keep the ones that work for you and let go of those that don't.

Conclusion

If you do everything, or even just focus on one of those chunks of time each day for one week, you'll feel like a new person. So, although you may feel like your hands are full, trust me that if and when you take action, you'll begin living your best life, regardless of circumstance.

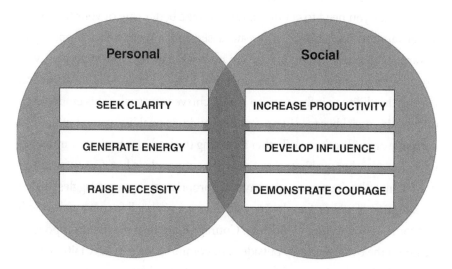

Here is a blueprint I give my students. We call these six habits the HP6. They have to do with clarity, energy, necessity, productivity, influence, and courage. They reflect what high performers do continually—from goal to goal, from project to project, from team to team, from person to person. The HP6 break down into these four steps, showing you how to accomplish all the things I gave as ways to optimize your day:

1. Seek Clarity (Vison)
2. Align Your Vibration
3. Remember Your WHY
4. Focused Deep Work (Get in Flow)

To build sustainable success you have to begin by breaking the habit of being your old self. That means replacing bad habits with good ones. If eating healthier is your goal, you won't stock your pantry with junk food. Instead, by building momentum in a positive direction, you'll prioritize seeking clarity. Do this and you'll be generating more energy than you've ever had. But when you begin to falter and lose focus, what you have to do next is raise necessity. This means raising the priorities of your daily routines from a good idea to an absolute need.

Perhaps you need to get out of debt or take better care of your family. By understanding the stakes, you create a sense of urgency that propels you toward greater productivity. There are numerous ways to boost productivity, like adopting healthy habits as I shared. But it's also about building influence. Having the ability to influence also helps achieve your goals. This empowered mindset is crucial because in professional and personal life, you often need to persuade or guide others. Whether it's taking the lead on a project or influencing colleagues, being able to positively impact people is key. Conversely, you don't want to be the person who says inappropriate things or struggles to gain the attention of others. Developing influence is a vital skill for personal growth and for becoming a high performer. Courage is another essential component. Summon the courage to step outside your comfort zone and have faith in your abilities. This is fundamental for performing at your best.

Cultivating positive habits and rituals is essential in your journey toward success. You need to envision your future, set exciting goals, and infuse energy through your personal and professional activities. Your ability to influence and inspire others also plays a crucial role in your journey. Remember the influential people in your life and strive to be a positive force in the lives of others. Be brave enough to step out of your comfort zone and believe in your capabilities.

The secret to building great habits lies in crafting a system. That's why I laid it all out for you in an achievable way. This system becomes your guiding force that shapes your actions every single day. While short-term goals could change from time to time, a system keeps you focused on your long-term growth. By incorporating these habits and rituals into your life,

REPLACE HABITS

NETFLIX MARATHONS	>>>	SLEEP
FAST-FOOD	>>>	HOMEMADE FOOD
TOXIC FRIENDS	>>>	MENTORS
TV	>>>	EXERCISE
COMPLAINING	>>>	GRATITUDE
BLAME	>>>	RESPONSIBILITY
OVERTHINKING	>>>	ACTION

you allow yourself to break free from old patterns, adopt beneficial habits, and maintain a growth mindset. You have within you the power to be the best version of yourself and achieve extraordinary success.

In the next chapter I will give you my Five-Step Manifestation Success Framework. This is the last thing you need to become an extraordinary human, able to create change in all areas of your life. That's true power.

Then, we will dive into the dynamic world of the IT ecosystem. Stay present through these sections to build the necessary foundation. This prepares you to fully apply the nine steps to building a successful career in the booming field of IT. Remember, it's not just about reading this book; it's about taking action and applying what you learn.

Remember, every small step counts. So just keep moving forward. My number one value that I live by as I strive for greatness is the concept of Kaizen. This means change for the better (also known as continuous improvement). The concept is simple: If I can improve by 1 percent every day, that is 365 percent in one year's time. I could, and next year will, write a whole book on this concept. But I'm planting the seed here so you too can harvest the fruits of cultivating it into your own life.

Bonus

I want to tell you about a book that was super transformative for me, especially when I was going through a rough patch. It's called *Think and Grow Rich*, by Napoleon Hill (TarcherPerigee, 2007). It was recommended by a close friend and was the first book I finished from beginning to end. Reading it during a period when I was very down and spiraling into negativity, it completely shifted my mindset.

Once you've delved into *Think and Grow Rich* (which covers personal growth and mindset), I suggest moving on to *High Performance Habits*, by Brendon Burchard (Hay House Inc., 2017). This book teaches you the habits you need to become a high performer—consistently, and without burnout. It dispels the notion that high performance means driving yourself into the ground. There are ways to perform at peak levels consistently without sacrificing balance in your life. It's a highly recommended read.

Here's a pro tip: Listen to these on Audible and even listen to them at 1.2X speed to get through them even faster while still retaining the key information.

CHAPTER FOUR

FIVE-STEP MANIFESTATION SUCCESS FRAMEWORK

"Never give up on a dream just because of the time it will take to accomplish it. The time will pass anyway."
— Earl Nightingale, American author

INTRODUCTION

Do you think it's possible to achieve everything you desire in your life? In the previous chapters, I've shown you how gratitude, a growth mindset, good habits, and powerful rituals are key in achieving your goals. Now, in this chapter I'm going to simplify even deeper layers of how to create a life you're proud of via the Five-Step Manifestation Success Framework. Using it will lead to a more fulfilling professional and personal life. Guaranteed.

Manifestation is more than just a buzzword; it's a powerful process that involves aligning your thoughts, emotions, and actions to create the reality you desire and deserve. As soon as you learn to manifest instantly, you take charge of your destiny.

The beauty of this framework is its practicality. It's not just some abstract concept; it's a proven set of actions you can start using right now, just like thousands of my students before you have done. Whether it's securing that dream job, forming stronger relationships, or just finding daily joy, this paves the way. Personal freedom, financial success, a healthier lifestyle, a yearly vacation . . . it's all within reach. To have all this, and so much more, stop leaving your goals and dreams to chance and start actively creating the life you want.

This framework is not just for your career; it's a life skill. Think about what it would mean for you (and your loved ones) if you could consistently create positive outcomes in every area of life. Let's harness this power together and get started!

THE FRAMEWORK: DREAM, BELIEVE, CREATE, EXECUTE, FOCUS

This idea of dreaming, creating a vision for yourself, getting motivated, and building ambition is not just word salad—it's something you can do on purpose, with purpose, and create a life you love. Or you can manifest on autopilot and stay in loops of unfulfillment, frustration, burnout . . . basically a downward spiral that is endless. Lucky for you, this framework shows you how to stay on the upward spiral.

There are five stages and they happen in sequential order. We restart the stages every time we start something new, dream of something big, have an aha! moment, or during an identify shift. As I shared from my own story, I went from being in a gang to dreaming of being a famous DJ. Then my dream shifted to being a rock-solid provider for my unborn baby. I went from dream to dream to dream, but only after I believed did things begin to really take shape.

Let's look at each stage.

Dream

Building a better future all starts with having a dream. Then, once you dream your dream, you start having clarity around it. Maybe it's having a vision of a better future for yourself, your spouse, your family, your coworkers, your children, or even your great-grandchildren. It could be a lifestyle that you want to live. Regardless, you just need to be able to dream of that better future, and you have to be optimistic. You've got to watch out because a lot of people are negative. That can put you in a downward spiral, muddying your vision and delegitimizing your dream. But you have to be confident in your dream, no matter what others say. Only you can dream your own dream of that better future and only you can see your vision entirely through. So, don't seek validation from others but search deep within and dream with your heart and mind aligned.

Believe

As I said, it starts with a dream, but once you see it, you have to believe it. A lot of people dream, but they never truly believe. And that's the problem. If you don't believe in yourself, then how can anyone else believe in you? I can't truly mentor you if you don't believe in yourself. I can lay out the entire pathway for you to build an amazing career in IT, but if you don't have a dream that you vividly imagine, you're on your own. If you don't believe you can make it happen, you may as well stop now until you're ready to go all in. It doesn't matter if I tell you that it's possible if you don't believe it. You need to believe in yourself. Once you are able to truly believe that it is possible, it becomes possible.

Remember the story of Roger Bannister? Before he broke the 4-minute mile, no one thought it was possible. That same year, over 30 other runners started breaking through that barrier because they believed that it was possible too. You can go to Glassdoor.com, Dice.com, or CareerBuilder.com to find all kinds of high-paying jobs that are widely available. CyberSeek.org is also a great resource to see hundreds of thousands of job openings all across the United States. There's no shortage of IT jobs that can give you the life you desire and pay the salary you've been dreaming of.

However, dreaming leaves you vulnerable to disappointment. I get it. I've been there. At a young age, I never thought I could actually break six figures, because up until then I never believed in myself or knew anyone who did it. I never believed for the sake of it because I had nothing to lose and so much to gain. It was always a burning desire to become the future version of myself. I believed so strongly, and I believed in myself achieving success no matter what. When I saw someone else who embodied who I wanted to become, I would say to myself, "They did it, and so can I." However, as your confidence gets bigger and you accomplish more in life, your dreams can become the "impossible" or "never-been-done" kind of dreams. That's when you can start to dream really big! It all begins with a smaller dream, and then the dreams get bigger over time.

Create

Once you believe, you can create your own path. You need to create a business plan of action. Put down what steps you need to do to get from point A to point B. I like to plan 18 months or 6 quarters out while also staying open to adjusting the plan as things shift.

Once the plan is formulated, you can move to the next step with clarity. With a self-defined action plan to get where you want to be, you'll create your own destiny. The chapters on mindset, habits, and rituals gave you plenty of action steps that you can use to transform dreams into reality. It's truly quite profound. Manifestation is more than just a concept; it's an empowering process that requires you to uplevel your thoughts, emotions, and actions to create the reality you desire.

The art of this phase is being specific with the endless possibilities of what you want to create, how you want to do it, and why. But those who dare to create must overcome the fear of failure. Fear of failure can freeze people into inaction for their entire lives. But that's not you. You know what you have to do.

Fundamentally, the creation phase is about seeing that vision, forming a plan that you can execute, and not fearing failure. Remember, failure (to someone with a growth mindset) is good—necessary even.

Execute

Taking massive action without the fear of failing is the key!

At NGT Academy, we have a proven blueprint system that you execute in less than 4 months that provides the results desired. Why? Because it's a plan that's been tried and tested thousands of times without failure.

Thomas Edison once said, "Vision without execution is delusion." What I want for you is to dream without limitations. Then, believe in yourself and your path fully, and create without fear of failure. But creation requires ambition. So, how do you build up ambition? You have to dream without limitation. Right now, begin writing down your dreams without limitation or holding back.

Most people don't dare to hope because of the pain of not getting what they want. This is the definition of being a coward. That's not you, at least not anymore. You have to remove every single self-limiting belief that you've had. What stops us from manifesting is bad thinking, bad habits, bad relationships, fear, fear of loss or pain, and of course, fear of failing. I know this because I've experienced all of this. When I failed my Cisco certification exam three times in a row, I had fear of judgment, fear of loss, shame . . . you name it.

So ask yourself, "What would I do if I was able to overcome all of my problems? Who would I be if I knew that my dream would become a reality one day? What would I do with this new success, joy, and opportunity?"

Maybe you can't even ask yourself those questions right now because you're just now opening up to taking real action on your dreams. Maybe you're complacent with just paying the bills and getting along. Maybe you're stuck in a situation and think you've just been dealt the wrong hand.

In the game of no-limit Texas Hold 'em, everyone gets two cards dealt by the dealer. Someone might be dealt a worse starting hand when someone else might be holding pocket aces. However, this does not mean anything until the full game is played out. What we call the flop, turn, and river still has to be dealt. Although we cannot change the cards we are dealt, we can change the way we play the hand and can still win with belief, strategy, and willpower. This is a perfect metaphor for the game of life as well. Don't be a victim and use that as an excuse to not play the hand you're dealt to live your life to its fullest potential to see and feel your way to victory!

It doesn't matter what hand you've been dealt. It's about how you play those cards. Only by playing them do you get rid of them and open yourself to being dealt a new hand. Millions of people keep the hand they're dealt and just deal with it. To be blunt, that's the stupidest thing someone can do. That's not who you are because that's not how to go from Zero to Engineer.

You have everything you need to change the way you live your life, carve out your destiny, and open up to your future. You can start right here, right now. And be kind to yourself amidst going through pain and suffering that can come with chasing your dream. Remember, that is all just a normal part of the process. But one day, you'll realize it was all worth it, and for that, you'll be grateful. Gratitude that comes through the fires of transformation is a joy no one can take away from you.

Focus

FOCUS stands for: Follow On Course Until Successful. Why? Because people give up way too easily since they are not committed to the seeing the process through. We live in a world full of distractions, all of which are trying to influence us or distract us from what we really want to do.

> *"All our dreams can come true, if we have the courage to pursue them."*
>
> — *Walt Disney*

This step requires discipline and consistency to see your vision all the way through. If your "why" is not strong enough, then it will be easy to pivot or simply give up right when you are about to break through.

I remember a guy I met while I was studying intently for my Cisco CCNA certification exam and I failed three times. I almost gave up, but I met John at an IT bootcamp training course in Dallas. He told me he failed the CCNA 12 TIMES!!! He almost gave up, but passed on this 13th attempt. He went from making $60,000 to $180,000 overnight. Moral of John's story: FOCUS. *And don't give up!*

65

CHAPTER SUMMARY, EXERCISES, AND CONCLUSION

Summary

Achieving your aspirations in the IT industry involves more than hard work and skills; it requires a clear vision and a method to turn that vision into reality. This chapter introduced the Five-Step Manifestation Success Framework, designed to help IT professionals clearly define their goals and systematically achieve them. By applying these principles, you can shape your career path and bring your professional dreams to life.

Step 1: Define Your Vision

The first step in the manifestation process is to have a clear and detailed vision of what you want to achieve. This involves more than just general desires; it requires a specific, vivid picture of your end goals.

- **Visualization Techniques**: Practice visualizing your career goals daily. Imagine yourself in your ideal job role, complete with details about the environment, responsibilities, and achievements.
- **Goal Setting**: Write down your career objectives using the SMART (Specific, Measurable, Achievable, Relevant, Time-bound) goal criteria to ensure they are well defined and actionable.

Step 2: Believe in Your Ability

Belief in your ability to achieve your goals is crucial. This belief acts as the fuel that powers your journey from aspiration to reality.

- **Affirmations**: Develop and recite positive affirmations related to your capabilities and goals. For example, "I am a skilled and respected software engineer who delivers innovative solutions."
- **Overcoming Doubts**: Identify any self-doubt or limiting beliefs that could hinder your progress. Address these doubts through further education and mentorship, and by reinforcing your past successes.

Step 3: Align Your Actions

Your daily actions must align with your long-term goals. This step is about breaking down your ultimate objectives into actionable tasks and integrating them into your daily routine.

- **Action Planning**: Create a detailed plan that outlines the steps needed to achieve your goals. This plan should include daily, weekly, and monthly tasks that progress toward your larger objectives (you can refer to the "Kaizen Stepping Stones" exercise in Chapter 2, "From Zero to Hero: The Mindset You Need to Succeed in IT").
- **Time Management**: Use tools and techniques to prioritize your tasks effectively, ensuring that each action contributes directly to your career goals.

Step 4: Overcome Obstacles

Challenges and setbacks are inevitable, but how you handle them can significantly impact your success. Developing strategies to overcome these obstacles is essential.

- **Problem-Solving Skills**: Enhance your problem-solving skills by studying common challenges in your field and how successful professionals have overcome them.

- **Resilience Building**: Strengthen your resilience by facing small challenges head-on and learning from each experience. This practice will prepare you for bigger hurdles.

Step 5: Receive and Adapt

As you work toward your goals, opportunities and offers will begin to manifest. It's important to be open to receiving them and flexible enough to adapt your plans as necessary.

- **Opportunity Recognition**: Develop the ability to recognize when an opportunity aligns with your goals and be prepared to act swiftly to capitalize on it.
- **Feedback and Adaptation**: Regularly solicit feedback on your progress and be willing to make adjustments to your plans based on constructive criticism and changing circumstances.

Exercises

Vision Board Creation

Objective: To visualize your dreams and reinforce your focus on specific goals.
Instructions:

- Gather magazines, online images, or drawing tools.
- Create a vision board highlighting your career, lifestyle, and personal goals. Include images, keywords, and affirmations that resonate with your dreams.
- Place it somewhere visible, like your desk or phone wallpaper, to keep your vision top of mind.

The Focus Window Technique

Objective: To build discipline and eliminate distractions while working toward your goals.

Instructions:

- Set a "focus window" of 25–30 minutes using a timer or app (e.g., Pomodoro).
- Work on tasks related to your roadmap without interruptions. After each session, take a 5-minute break.
- Gradually increase the number of focus windows per day to strengthen your execution ability.

Opportunity Response Simulation

Objective: To enhance decision-making skills and ensure alignment between opportunities and career goals.

Instructions:

- Choose 3–5 realistic scenarios (e.g., a job offer, freelance project, or certification program) related to your career path.
- Role-play these scenarios with a partner or mentor. If a partner isn't available, write your responses as if addressing an interviewer or recruiter.
- Use the STAR method (Situation, Task, Action, Result) to assess how each opportunity aligns with your short- and long-term goals.
- Reflect: After each simulation, discuss or journal what went well and how you can improve your response in future scenarios.

Monthly Progress Check-In

Objective: To stay on track with goals by evaluating progress, addressing obstacles, and making necessary adjustments.

Instructions:

- Schedule 30–60 minutes at the end of each month to assess your progress toward career milestones and personal goals.
- Use a structured agenda to cover key areas:

- What milestones did I achieve?
- Where did I struggle, and why?
- What adjustments can I make for next month?
- If possible, include a mentor or accountability partner in these meetings for additional insights and feedback.
- Record any new insights or action steps in a journal or tracker to build continuity month-to-month.

Strategic Educational Investments

Objective: To ensure continuous growth by strategically selecting courses, workshops, or certifications aligned with your goals.

Instructions:

- Identify two key skill areas you need to develop (e.g., cloud computing or leadership) based on industry trends and personal aspirations.
- Research available learning options (free or paid) like NGT Academy, Coursera, Udemy, or industry-specific bootcamps.
- Develop a learning schedule for the year, allocating time monthly or weekly for courses or certifications.
- After completing each course, apply your new skills in a project or practice setting to solidify learning.
- Keep a learning log to track completed courses, certifications, and how they impact your career progress.

Conclusion

As we close out this chapter, I want you to remember that life is a journey, and the path you choose to follow is up to you. The Five-Step Manifestation Success Framework that I've outlined in this chapter—Dream, Believe, Create, Execute, and Focus—is a road map for your journey, regardless of the destination.

However, as with everything you've read, it is useful only if you actually use it. This framework is not a one-size-fits-all solution. It's a guide, a set of principles that need to be lived, internalized, and applied consistently to yield the results you seek.

Bringing your dreams into reality requires an unwavering commitment to yourself. You need to dream big, believe in yourself and your capabilities, create your own path, execute your plans without fear, and above all, stay focused on your goals no matter the obstacles.

Remember, you are not alone in this journey. I've been there too, and just like you, I've had to overcome my doubts and fears to achieve the dreams that once seemed impossible to me. This process is not easy, but it's worth every moment. Trust me. When you start landing six-figure offers, having more time and money to travel, and living an elevated life, you'll know it's been more than worth it.

Don't forget that this framework is not only about professional success; it's about personal achievement as well. You have the power to create a life you're proud of, one that brings joy and satisfaction in all areas, not just your career.

Now, are you ready to make a change? If you are, brace yourself, because I'm about to challenge a common belief that holds so many people back. You'll learn how it is entirely possible, and indeed practical, to learn the industry in just 4 months, not 4 years. It's time to question the status quo, redefine your path, and step boldly into your dream future. Are you ready to take the leap?

CHAPTER FIVE

COLLEGE IS *NOT* THE ANSWER: LEARN THE INDUSTRY IN 4 MONTHS, NOT 4 YEARS

"The secret of getting ahead is getting started."

— Mark Twain

INTRODUCTION

If you knew that you wanted to break into IT, would you spend 4 years in college or make it happen in less than 4 months? I think the answer is obvious. Like many others, I also thought that a college degree was essential for landing high-paying IT job offers. However, after getting my dream job without a college degree, I realized that the "higher education" system is completely broken. Why pay huge sums of money to be taught in ways that lack critical thinking and not be given the truly useful training and industry secrets to be a high-performing IT professional?

Unless you want to become a doctor, a lawyer, or the like, going to college is the biggest lie that we've been told, but with IT engineering, you can learn through hands-on practical skills training and mentorship, as you'll see in this book. That's why I'm going to give you the nine steps to demand six-figure job offers from top Fortune 500 companies. We're going to talk about multiple things that make a college degree irrelevant, making you more competent and more qualified than any college graduate!

After achieving the American Dream and going from Zero to Engineer without college, I realized I had a bigger problem to solve and a bigger impact to make. That's when and why I created NGT Academy. I was astounded to see that people were paying over $120,000 for a 4-year degree just to work in network administration—or not even land a job in the industry due to their lack of competence and hands-on experience. That's obviously so pointless to me. Why? Because I knew that I could train individuals to be junior-level engineers in just 4 months. Being an instructor in the U.S. Air Force with a Top Secret clearance, I was teaching 18-to-22-year-olds to become network/cyber operations professionals in 4 months. How do you think the military would scale recruiting and training if they had to send all their recruits to college for 4 years before they deployed them in the field? See, it's quite obvious.

Saying "No" to College Is Saying "Yes" to Success

A 4-year college education is absolutely not necessary to break into nearly all of the best careers across all industries. Why? Because half of the college curriculum consists of general studies such as history, math, creative writing, and other classes that don't pertain to your career. And that's 2 full years into it! And then the other 2 years, you barely get any hands-on training. As a result, you leave college with a huge debt, no confidence, and skills that aren't appealing to employers. Sure, you show you can stick something through and graduate, but with NGT Academy, you show them the same thing with all the essential skills and certifications.

The college system is broken and out of date. If there is any practical training, it's based on theories and concepts, often taught by individuals who have never worked in the IT field or data centers. It's a scam! It's better to learn from the military's approach. The military trains individuals in specific roles such as jet mechanics, logistics professionals, or intelligence specialists within months through focused and effective training. The military trains you to be job ready, and they do it in a few months. That's truly what the employers want—job-ready candidates who are competent in a particular range of skill sets with the focus. It also shows you have the responsibility to get the job done, and get it done correctly, the first time.

Learning from this, I established NGT Academy to provide people from super diverse backgrounds with the training they need to become IT professionals. Our curriculum was created by Jacob Hess, my cofounder, and me after training thousands of military personnel. Following a skills-first and project-based learning approach, we built our programs with a similar format to how we trained in the military. In addition to knowledge-based training, we train on real-world skills, build robust lab environments, roll out multiple capstone projects, and perform skills qualification checks along the way. With this methodology, students are well trained and job ready, setting up people who are just like you for success.

As an IT professional, you need hands-on training to develop essential skills. Just like becoming a barber or mechanic, you don't need 4 years in college studying unrelated subjects. You need practical experience that you can gain in trade schools in just a few months. If you're training to be a bartender, you don't want to be deep in books, theories, and concepts just reading about cocktails. No! You need to know how to actually make the cocktails and how to make them taste good. For instance, my mother became a bartender after taking a short course and absolutely crushing an on-the-job interview. Hands-on experience is going to level you up faster than anything else because it builds competence and gives you the confidence to break into the actual job.

It works the same way for the IT field. I learned invaluable skills by building my first PC. No books or theories; I dove straight in. I bought the computer case, the motherboard, the hard drive, the computer brains, the CPU, and the cables and put everything together to understand how a computer works. Then, I connected it to the Internet and the network to understand how it communicates. When you have two or more devices connected, that creates a network. That's what the World Wide Web is—a series of devices all interconnected, talking to one another. Only when you get hands-on experience are you able to understand at a high level what all these devices do.

Understanding some of the concepts and theories behind computer technology is vital but should not be the primary focus. Colleges mainly focus on theories, while practical training takes a backseat. However, like the military, NGT Academy employs an 80–20 rule, focusing 80 percent on hands-on training and 20 percent on theories. The skills we give our students are rock-solid, giving them the confidence and competence to perform on the job.

Getting the skills to become job ready is far more important than a fancy degree. I know you can see through the misconception that college is the only path to a successful career in IT. But to make it even clearer, the upcoming chapters will reveal the shortest, most effective way to enter and prosper in the IT sector. The beauty of this field is that with online resources, you can acquire skills from anywhere in the world.

CHAPTER SUMMARY, EXERCISES, AND CONCLUSION

Summary

In today's rapidly evolving tech landscape, traditional 4-year college degrees are often not the most efficient or cost-effective way to launch a successful career in IT. This chapter explored alternative educational pathways that can equip you with the necessary skills and knowledge in a fraction of the time and cost. You learned how focused training programs, certifications, bootcamps, and self-directed learning can propel you into the IT industry quickly and effectively.

Rethinking Traditional Education

Traditional university programs can provide a broad educational foundation but often lack the specificity and practical experience needed for immediate effectiveness in IT roles. Moreover, the tech industry evolves so quickly that much of the knowledge gained in a 4-year program can become outdated.

- **Cost vs. Benefit Analysis:** Examine the rising costs of college tuition and evaluate the ROI by comparing employment rates, starting salaries, and the real-world applicability of skills learned. Research from platforms like CyberSeek and Salary.com helps determine how certifications compare in cost and salary outcomes.
- **Speed to Market:** Explore how faster training programs can help you start your career sooner, reducing opportunity costs and allowing you to gain experience quickly.

Alternative Education Pathways

Alternative education options are more focused on practical, job-ready skills and allow learners to adapt quickly to industry trends.

- **Certification Programs:** Certifications like CompTIA, Cisco's CCNA, and AWS Certified Solutions Architect are industry-recognized benchmarks that validate relevant IT knowledge.
- **Engineering Bootcamps or Vocational Schools:** Research the intensive, immersive learning environments of bootcamps or vocational schools such as those provided by NGT Academy that focus on the most current and in-demand IT skills and technologies that you can master by working on real-world IT projects to be job ready in months, not years.
- **Online Courses, Bootcamps, and Massive Open Online Courses (MOOCs):** Platforms such as Coursera, Udemy, Pluralsight, and LinkedIn Learning offer courses designed by industry experts, frequently updated to reflect market trends.
- **Apprenticeships and Internships:** Hands-on roles in companies offer practical experience and networking opportunities, often acting as a direct pathway into full-time employment.

Building a Customized Learning Path

Creating a personalized learning path ensures that education aligns with individual career goals, strengths, and timelines.

- **Assessing Personal and Career Goals:** Start by identifying long-term career objectives and assessing current skills. Tools like a gap analysis help pinpoint areas for improvement.
- **Choosing the Right Programs:** Select programs based on quality, relevance, and delivery format. Research course content, instructor credentials, and graduate outcomes.

- **Combining Different Learning Modalities:** Combine various learning modalities (online courses, bootcamps, self-study) to create a comprehensive and practical educational experience.

Leveraging Learning for Career Advancement

Once skills are acquired, using them strategically can accelerate career growth.

- **Portfolio Development:** Create a portfolio showcasing completed projects, certifications, and case studies that demonstrate competence. This is a key differentiator in the job market.
- **Networking and Professional Visibility:** Use platforms like LinkedIn to connect with professionals, join industry forums, and actively engage with tech communities to build your professional brand.
- **Continuous Learning and Upgrading:** Commit to lifelong learning by pursuing advanced certifications or staying up-to-date with evolving technologies like AI, cloud computing, or cybersecurity.

Exercises

Education Path Planner

Objective: Create a structured plan to pursue education efficiently.
Instructions:

- Identify certifications, courses, bootcamps, and other training relevant to your career goals.
- Estimate costs and time commitments for each.
- Create a timeline with clear milestones (e.g., "Earn AWS Solutions Architect in 6 months").
- Include contingency plans in case timelines shift.
- Update the plan quarterly based on progress and new learning opportunities.

Industry Engagement Plan

Objective: Leverage networking opportunities to stay informed and connected with industry professionals.

Instructions:

- Research and list two or more conferences, webinars, or networking events to attend this year.
- Prepare by following speakers on LinkedIn or reviewing recent industry reports to engage meaningfully in conversations.
- After each event, connect with at least three people you met and write down key insights to apply in your career.
- Bonus: Join online communities (e.g., Reddit IT forums, LinkedIn groups) to stay engaged year-round.

Certification Roadmap

Objective: Strategically select and pursue certifications that align with your career trajectory.

Instructions:

- List certifications relevant to your desired field (e.g., CCNA for networking, AWS for cloud).
- Prioritize certifications based on industry demand and your career path.
- Create a road map, specifying timelines for exam preparation, practice, and completion.
- Set up a system to track progress (e.g., habit tracker, checklist) and reward milestones achieved.

Cost vs. Benefit Analysis Exercise

Objective: Evaluate the financial return on investment (ROI) of various educational paths to make an informed decision about your career in IT.

Instructions:

1. **Research Tuition Costs vs. Certification Costs:**
   - Compare the costs of a 4-year degree program (tuition, fees, etc.) with certifications such as CompTIA, AWS, or Cisco's CCNA.
   - Use tools like CollegeBoard for tuition data and CyberSeek for certification costs and demand in the job market.

2. **Compare Employment Rates and Starting Salaries:**
   - Explore job portals like Glassdoor, LinkedIn, or CyberSeek to review starting salaries for degree holders versus certification holders in your target IT field.
   - Use Salary.com to compare average salaries for entry-level and senior roles requiring different credentials.

3. **Assess Real-World Skill Application:**
   - Identify skills taught in degree programs versus those in certifications. Analyze job descriptions on sites like CyberSeek to see which skills and certifications align with industry demand.

4. **Create a Cost-Benefit Table:**
   - List degrees and certifications you are considering with the following metrics:
     Tuition/Certification Cost | Time to Complete | Expected Salary | Job Market Demand | Hands-On Skills Provided

5. **Summarize Your Findings:**
   - Based on your comparison, write a brief report highlighting which path (or combination) offers the best ROI for your career goals. Consider both short-term and long-term financial and learning outcomes.

Conclusion

As of July 2024, there are over 469,930 open IT and cybersecurity jobs in the United States (check out the heatmap at www.cyberseek.org/heatmap.html), with over one million cloud engineer jobs to be created by the end of 2024, according to market research firm IDC (https://thinkcloudly.com/blogs/cloud/one-million-cloud-computing-jobs-by-2024). With the advancement in technology, particularly artificial intelligence, there is a consistent demand for IT professionals. Across the globe, there are several million open jobs in IT and the number is ever growing. With AI and automation, there's going to be a lot of displaced workers. This is the time to build skill sets in computers and information technology, because there will be a growing demand for those jobs. We cannot fill these IT jobs faster than the students coming out of the broken college education system. That's why we built the Academy, giving people the essential skills they need to quickly get high-paying careers.

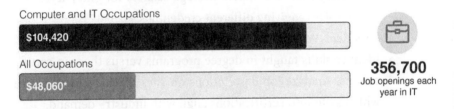

Computer and IT Occupations

$104,420

All Occupations

$48,060*

356,700
Job openings each
year in IT

Source: US Bureau of Labor Statistics – 2023.

Not only is the American Dream real, but I also truly believe technology is the gateway to financial freedom and to building wealth for you, your family, and your loved ones. Whether you want to stay in IT as an engineer or a manager, move your way into an executive position, or even start your own company one day, this industry has limitless opportunities.

If you look at some of the top tech CEOs, they all started in IT or computer and information systems. You have Mark Cuban, who first started making PCs in his dorm room and then built his businesses through that entry point. You also have Michael Dell, who built custom PCs while in college and then founded Dell Computers. Look no further than Elon Musk, consistently one of the richest people in the world. He started in IT and now he's sending people and thousands of satellites into space.

I wish I had known all this when I began my IT career at the age of 21. It would have saved me years of trial and error. But that's exactly why everything that I've learned in my career, spanning two decades, is condensed in this book. This information will save you time, money, and effort in achieving your dream job and financial freedom. The American Dream is real and accessible, and a career in technology is a highly lucrative opportunity for anyone who's willing to make it happen.

CHAPTER SIX

UNDERSTANDING THE ENTIRE IT ECOSYSTEM

"Impossible is just an opinion."
— Paulo Coelho, Brazilian lyricist and novelist

INTRODUCTION

Billions of dollars are circulated within the IT ecosystem, and the IT team is at the center of it all. Why? Because the IT team is the heartbeat of this lucrative industry. This is because IT is the tech that's fueling this multitrillion-dollar sector. As an IT professional, you could have a role anywhere within this vast ecosystem.

So, let me explain. The IT team oversees the technology, implementation, maintenance, and support for businesses with a significant number of employees. Therefore, any company with more than 50 or 100 employees will eventually hire one or two IT professionals, or they will outsource their entire IT team to a managed service provider.

Why does this matter? The IT team is tasked with distributing all the laptops, computers, and printers; establishing and securing the network; managing the firewall; setting up wireless access control; and installing cloud applications for newly hired employees. The IT team maintains the entire technological infrastructure. The team includes frontline support, the help desk, server administrators, infrastructure managers, and a team leader, who may be an IT director or VP, depending on the size of the IT team. The composition of your IT team will depend on your company's reliance on cloud apps and the size of the organization. Larger organizations may adopt both cloud and on-premises solutions, requiring distinct business units within the IT team to manage various infrastructures effectively.

Not every company requires programmers. In tech hubs like Silicon Valley, there's a significant demand for software engineers and programmers. These professionals might be part of an IT team, but they usually work separately. These teams are typically responsible for building the apps. So, you could work for Twitter/X Corp. as a software engineer because they would need many engineers to develop their own software.

However, many companies outsource their software, opting for software as a service (SaaS) or buying software from large enterprises. These companies don't need programmers because software is sold to them by manufacturers. For instance, when I worked in customer service at a credit union, I was part of an IT team that didn't include any programmers.

I am convinced that regardless of whether you aim to be a network engineer, a cybersecurity analyst, a cloud engineer, an IT manager, or a software engineer, you should start within an IT team. Why? Because it lays a solid foundation. It provides an entry point and helps you figure out the direction you want your career to take. In Chapter 7, "IT Career Pathways,"

I'll explain why starting in an IT team and learning networking is the best way to build your IT career.

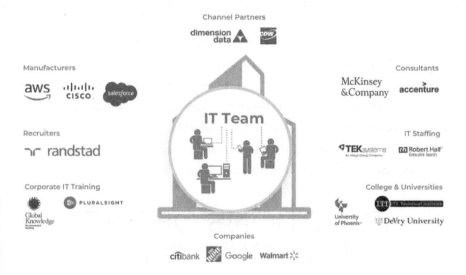

Now that we've discussed the ecosystem, understanding that the IT team at its core, whether you work for a Fortune 500 company or a small-to-medium enterprise, is essential in supporting the technology that the company relies on for its operations. The bigger the company, the better for you, because you'll be able to grow and demand a higher salary.

The IT team usually operates within a company under the guidance of a director, VP, or CIO who oversees the entire division. They might even use IT staffing firms to assemble their IT workforce. Companies like Dell often engage consultants for projects. Some small businesses will use managed service providers (MSPs) to fully outsource their IT requirements.

You will also find significant IT teams on the manufacturing side and within channel partner operations. I will discuss this more in Step 9 (discussed in Chapter 9, "Four More Steps to Demand Six-Figure Job Offers from Fortune 500 Companies"). But for now, understand that starting with an IT team at a company is your first step. If you want to fast-track your career, consider moving from the IT team into what I'd call the minor leagues, like working for an MSP or channel partner.

And, when you aspire to join the major leagues later in your career, consider working for a manufacturer like Cisco, SolarWinds, Palo Alto Networks, or Zoom. Any tech company, usually originating from Silicon Valley, with tens of thousands of customers and employees, would be what I consider the major leagues. Or you can go to work for the tens of thousands of companies that resell these technologies. They are called value-added resellers (which we cover in the nine steps).

This is an overview of the IT ecosystem. Grasping this ecosystem is vital because it helps you know how to navigate it effectively.

FUNCTIONS OF THE IT ECOSYSTEM

The IT ecosystem, encompassing technology, hardware, software, applications, and people, is the backbone that sustains an organization's IT operations. It's an indispensable part of the success of contemporary businesses, largely contributing to incredible innovations, as well as increasing efficiency and productivity.

One of the most important parts of the IT ecosystem is its role in supporting digital transformation. This transformation, built alongside the people who operate these systems, gives us access to cutting-edge technologies and tools. When you work in IT, you're helping humanity expand our potential like never before!

Efficiency is another hallmark of the IT ecosystem. Automation of mundane and repetitive tasks, streamlining of workflows, and enhanced communication channels enables businesses to operate with a higher degree of efficiency while simultaneously cutting financial and environmental costs. Collaboration, the foundation for all true success, is massively bolstered by the IT ecosystem. The endless tech, tools, and platforms it offers ensures that people can work together effectively, regardless of geographical barriers. It really is a World Wide Web.

Lastly, the IT ecosystem is innovation's number-one ally. Technologies like AI and the Internet of Things (IoT) provide endless ways to create new things, establish new connections, and transform our world with innovative tech. We're engineering novel products and services every single day, and by working in this field, you're the frontline superhero who gets to watch it all unfold.

However, it's super important to talk about how the IT ecosystem grapples with several hurdles in tackling cybersecurity threats. One of the biggest challenges is the growing sophistication of threats. Cyber attackers now use an array of tactics such as social engineering, malware, and phishing, making the defense mechanism more complicated for IT professionals. Also, IT infrastructure itself has evolved to become exceedingly complex, with an array of interconnected devices. This raises the difficulty in managing security, as the large number of connections increases the potential avenues for attack. Despite their user-friendliness, many devices lack robust security features, rendering them susceptible to attacks.

The widespread adoption of cloud computing, though beneficial, has also opened new security challenges. The security options of cloud providers might not always align with an organization's needs, making data stored on the cloud highly vulnerable.

But the absolute most significant issue in the industry is the shortage of skilled cybersecurity personnel. That means you are the best solution to all of these issues. As the demand for expertise exceeds how many people are trained to get into this booming industry, businesses find it tough to create and enforce efficient cybersecurity strategies.

Inside an organization, the threats might not always be external. There are instances of insider threats where a security compromise stems from employees or contractors, either unintentionally or with malice. This means that as an IT professional, you are an actual "cyber warrior," protecting the integrity of the system from internal and external threats. Without you, the entire system comes crashing down.

CHAPTER SUMMARY, EXERCISES, AND CONCLUSION

Summary

To truly excel in the field of IT, it is essential to understand the entire IT ecosystem. This ecosystem includes various sectors, technologies, and roles, and they interconnect to support and drive the digital world. This chapter provided a comprehensive overview of the IT ecosystem, helping you to navigate, specialize, and innovate within this dynamic field.

The Structure of the IT Ecosystem

The IT ecosystem is vast and complex, composed of numerous components that interact in various ways. Understanding this structure is crucial for anyone looking to build a successful career in IT.

Core Components

These form the backbone of IT infrastructure, ensuring that businesses can operate smoothly:

- **Hardware:** Physical devices like computers, servers, networking equipment, and IoT devices.
- **Software:** Applications and operating systems that power these devices.

- **Networks:** Communication frameworks that connect hardware and software systems, allowing seamless data flow.
- **Data:** The lifeblood of the ecosystem, enabling organizations to make decisions, run operations, and provide services.

Example: A healthcare provider's IT infrastructure involves network-connected computers and cloud systems for accessing patient records while cybersecurity tools protect sensitive health data.

Emerging Technologies

As technology evolves, new innovations reshape the IT landscape:

- **AI and Machine Learning:** Automate processes and enable predictive analytics. AI-based chatbots improve customer service, while machine learning models analyze data for insights.
- **Big Data Analytics:** Manage large datasets, helping organizations identify trends and make informed decisions.
- **Blockchain:** Strengthens security and transparency, especially in financial services and supply chains.
- **IoT (Internet of Things):** Connects devices, enhancing automation and smart city infrastructure.

Example: Smart cities use IoT sensors to monitor traffic patterns, reducing congestion through real-time data analysis.

Service Providers

IT service providers ensure businesses run efficiently, offering a range of solutions:

- **Cloud Services:** Companies like Amazon Web Services (AWS) and Microsoft Azure offer infrastructure as a service (IaaS), platform as a service (PaaS), and software as a service (SaaS).

- **Managed Service Providers (MSPs):** Handle IT operations for businesses, from network management to cybersecurity.
- **Consulting Firms:** Provide expert advice and help organizations implement new technologies.

Example: A company might use Salesforce's SaaS platform for customer relationship management (CRM) and outsource its network security to an MSP.

Key Sectors within the IT Industry

Understanding these sectors can guide you toward a specialization that aligns with your career goals:

- **Telecommunications:** Provides the infrastructure for data transmission through networks, crucial for everything from mobile communication to cloud access.
- **Software Development:** Involves creating applications and software systems using methodologies like Agile and DevOps.
- **Cybersecurity:** Focuses on protecting systems from digital threats, such as malware or phishing attacks, with growing demand for specialists.
- **Health IT:** Involves managing health information systems, telemedicine platforms, and electronic health records (EHRs).

Roles and Career Pathways

Navigating roles within the IT ecosystem helps professionals choose relevant career paths:

- **Technical Roles:** Include network engineers, software developers, and data scientists, each requiring specific certifications and expertise.

- **Business and Management Roles:** Roles like IT project managers and CIOs require both technical knowledge and leadership skills.
- **Emerging Roles:** New roles, such as AI engineers, cloud architects, and cybersecurity analysts, are shaping the future of IT careers.

Real-Life Applications

Explore the real-world applications of the IT ecosystem to understand the practical impact of IT in various industries.

- **Case Study – Smart Cities:** Explore how IT ecosystems support the development of smart cities, focusing on integrated technologies like IoT, big data, and AI to enhance urban living.
- **Case Study – Fintech Innovations:** Analyze the role of IT in financial technologies, including mobile banking, blockchain, and cybersecurity measures that protect transactions.

Exercises

IT Ecosystem Map Creation

Objective: To visually understand the interconnected technologies, roles, and sectors within the IT ecosystem, aiding in identifying potential specialization areas.

Instructions:

1. Use mind-mapping tools like Lucidchart, Miro, or Draw.io to build a visual map of the IT ecosystem.
2. Identify core areas (hardware, software, networks, cloud, cybersecurity, etc.) and map how technologies and roles interrelate.
3. Highlight key technologies (e.g., cloud computing, cybersecurity) and industry sectors (telecom, healthcare IT, etc.) you're interested in.
4. Add potential career pathways under each sector, noting what skills and certifications are relevant.

5. Use this map as a dynamic resource, updating it as you explore further or learn about new technologies.

Technology Impact Analysis

Objective: Evaluate how an emerging technology can impact your career and the broader IT ecosystem.

Instructions:
1. Pick a new technology (e.g., AI, DevOps, or blockchain).
2. Google search or read summaries on Gartner, CyberSeek, or blogs to understand its potential growth and applications.
3. In a notebook or Word doc, answer:
   - What jobs or skills are connected to this technology?
   - How might it reshape IT roles?
4. Reflect on whether it aligns with your career goals.

Role Exploration Project

Objective: To deepen understanding of potential IT career paths, educational requirements, and daily responsibilities.

Instructions:
1. Select three IT roles you're interested in (e.g., cloud architect, cybersecurity analyst, DevOps engineer).
2. Use resources like LinkedIn, CompTIA, or the Bureau of Labor Statistics (BLS) to research:
   - Required education and certifications
   - Daily tasks and responsibilities
   - Career paths and salary ranges
3. Create a comparative chart to summarize your findings, focusing on similarities and differences between the roles.
4. Use this analysis to prioritize which role aligns best with your interests, skills, and long-term goals.

Sector Specialization Plan

Objective: Find an IT sector that matches your strengths and build a plan to enter it.

Instructions:
1. Choose a sector like healthcare IT, fintech, or telecommunications.
2. Identify at least two skills or certifications needed for this sector.
3. Create a 6-month plan to get started. For example:
   - Take one online course on Coursera.
   - Attend one webinar related to the sector.

Networking Strategy

Objective: Build a network of industry connections for career growth.

Instructions:
1. Set a goal to reach out to one professional per week on LinkedIn— start with a simple message like, "I admire your work in [field]. Do you have any advice for someone starting out?"
2. Join an online community (e.g., a LinkedIn group or Reddit forum) and engage in discussions.
3. Attend at least one virtual or in-person event every 3 months—look for meetups or webinars.

Conclusion

The opportunities within the IT ecosystem are enormous and continually growing. Let's put this into perspective with some eye-popping figures. Amazon is anticipated to rake in over $105.2 billion in revenue in 2024 through its AWS cloud offering alone. Back in 2012, Cisco, where I was working at the time, was generating around $40 billion in total sales. This comparison highlights just how much the industry has grown in the past decade.

The IT ecosystem is colossal, with hundreds of billions of dollars in IT products and technology solutions available, ranging from switches, routers, and firewalls to cloud services and software. These are all products created by tech manufacturers. And who are the customers for these products? The very heart of this ecosystem: the IT teams! They are the ones who purchase these products for their companies. As these manufacturers sell hundreds of billions of dollars' worth of solutions, it highlights the sheer scale of opportunities for learning and working with these technologies.

If you have a passion for technology and are eager to be part of an industry that's not just lucrative but also cutting-edge, there's no better time to dive into IT. The potential for growth is unlike any other industry, and as companies continue to invest in technology, the demand for skilled IT professionals will only continue to soar. In the next few chapters, I'll give you the necessary knowledge and skills; your six-figure career is right around the corner!

CHAPTER SEVEN

IT CAREER PATHWAYS

"The only way to do great work is to love what you do."

— Steve Jobs

INTRODUCTION

If you aspire to master algebra, you must first grasp the fundamentals of mathematics, such as the principles of addition, subtraction, division, and multiplication. Similarly, when starting an IT career, it's crucial to establish a solid foundation. This means acquainting yourself with the basic concepts of computer operations, gaining insights into high-level IT concepts, and starting out with an understanding of networking.

Networking is the foundation to break into any technology sector. Once you learn networking, you can understand and specialize in other advanced technologies. Cloud data centers, cybersecurity, systems engineering, DevOps, or any specializations are all constructed on the bedrock of networking. Even becoming a programmer or a software engineer builds on networking as the foundation. Why is this the case? It's simple. Without an understanding of how networks function, it's impossible to fully grasp these other technologies.

You may already see yourself working for a particular company, say Google, and maybe your aspiration is to be a top-tier engineer and architect there. Believe me; that is an ambitious dream. You're looking to construct the equivalent of a mansion, and for that, you need a blueprint to build it right the first time. To successfully build your dream, you must begin with a blueprint (which is this book). Then, you've got to lay a strong, rock-solid foundation and make sure there are no holes or cracks in the slab.

The more expansive and sturdier the foundation, the more remarkable the structure that can be built on it. With this analogy, you can think of the concrete slab as the networking foundation and building components of the house or rooms are all the special skills layered on top of your foundation. The stronger your networking foundation, the wider and bigger you can go with specializing in high-demand skill sets. I like to refer to this as the "technology stack." You have the potential to become what is known as a full-stack IT engineer. To put things into perspective, back in 2000 when I began my journey, I studied networking, secured a Cisco Certified Network Associate (CCNA) certification, and learned switching and routing. Given that Cisco Systems was essentially laying the groundwork for the Internet, you could easily land a job with a salary of $80,000 just by obtaining your CCNA.

That's how hot the Internet era was during its early days. Nowadays, we see similar trends with cloud technologies, cybersecurity, DevOps, and AI automation. It's crucial to recognize that first mastering networking should be the launchpad for various career paths, most of which offer six-figure salaries. In the next section, I'll outline the career opportunities, starting with the help desk all the way up to executive positions. For those eager to advance quickly, programs like NGT Academy can provide a pathway to skip the help desk and transition directly into engineering roles.

LIST OF IT POSITIONS

The list I'll provide generally reflects a progression in both experience and pay rates, with help desk technician an entry-level position and IT director or chief information officer (CIO) an executive-level position. However, it's important to note that salary can vary widely depending on various factors such as geographic location, the size of the company, the specific industry, and your individual qualifications.

Also, some roles like being an administrator or systems engineer don't follow a linear progression from other roles, as they may require specialized skills and expertise that can come with higher salaries even with relatively fewer years of experience compared to more common roles.

Software Development

- **Software Developer**
  - **Role Description:** Designs, codes, tests, and maintains software applications tailored to client or company requirements.
  - **Area of Specialization:** Software development
- **Front-End Developer**
  - **Role Description:** Focuses on the user interface and experience aspects of software and applications, implementing design principles and ensuring responsiveness across devices.
  - **Area of Specialization:** Software development
- **Back-End Developer**
  - **Role Description:** Handles the server-side logic, database interactions, and integration of the work front-end developers do.
  - **Area of Specialization:** Software development

- **Full-Stack Developer**
  - **Role Description:** Skilled in both front-end and back-end development, capable of handling all aspects of web application development.
  - **Area of Specialization:** Software development

Network and Systems Administration/Engineering

- **Network Administrator/Engineer**
  - **Role Description:** Manages and maintains network infrastructure, ensuring reliable network availability to users.
  - **Area of Specialization:** Network administration/engineering
- **Systems Administrator**
  - **Role Description:** Responsible for the upkeep, configuration, and reliable operation of computer systems, especially multiuser computers, such as servers.
  - **Area of Specialization:** Systems administration

Cybersecurity

- **Cybersecurity Analyst**
  - **Role Description:** Protects systems against cyber threats, analyzes security breaches, and restores systems to normal operation.
  - **Area of Specialization:** Cybersecurity
- **Penetration Tester**
  - **Role Description:** Simulates cyberattacks to identify vulnerabilities in security systems before they can be exploited maliciously.
  - **Area of Specialization:** Cybersecurity

Data Management and Analytics

- **Data Analyst**
  - **Role Description:** Analyzes data using statistical techniques to help companies make informed business decisions.
  - **Area of Specialization:** Data analytics

- **Data Scientist**
  - **Role Description:** Uses advanced analytics technologies, including machine learning and predictive modeling, to extract insights from datasets.
  - **Area of Specialization:** Data science

Cloud Computing

- **Cloud Architect**
  - **Role Description:** Designs and manages cloud computing strategies, including cloud adoption plans, cloud application design, and cloud management and monitoring.
  - **Area of Specialization:** Cloud computing
- **Cloud Engineer**
  - **Role Description:** Focuses on the technical aspects of cloud computing, including design, planning, management, maintenance, and support.
  - **Area of Specialization:** Cloud computing
- **DevOps Engineer**
  - **Role Description:** Facilitates collaboration between software development and IT operations teams to improve productivity and efficiency in software development processes.
  - **Area of Specialization:** Cloud computing

IT Support and Help Desk

- **Help Desk Technician**
  - **Role Description:** Provides technical support and troubleshooting services to end users who need assistance with their computer hardware or software.
  - **Area of Specialization:** Technical support

- **IT Support Specialist**
  - **Role Description:** Supports IT systems and users, resolves technical problems, and ensures that all IT needs of the organization are met.
  - **Area of Specialization:** Technical support

IT Management

- **IT Manager**
  - **Role Description:** Oversees an organization's technology infrastructure and the team that supports it, ensuring that systems are reliable and meet the needs of the business.
  - **Area of Specialization:** IT management
- **Chief Information Officer (CIO)**
  - **Role Description:** Defines IT strategy and policy, overseeing all aspects of an organization's IT operations and ensuring alignment with business objectives.
  - **Area of Specialization:** Executive management
- **Chief Technology Officer (CTO)**
  - **Role Description:** Focuses on scientific and technological issues within an organization, developing new technologies and managing technical teams.
  - **Area of Specialization:** Executive management

Project Management

- **IT Project Manager**
  - **Role Description:** Plans, initiates, and manages IT projects, leading teams that install or upgrade hardware, software, and networks.
  - **Area of Specialization:** Project management

Project Management

- **IT Project Manager**
  - **Role Description:** Plans, initiates, and manages IT projects, leading teams that install or upgrade hardware, software, and networks.
  - **Area of Specialization:** Project management

Emerging New IT Roles

- **AI Engineer**
  - **Role Description:** Develops AI models and algorithms to automate processes, analyze data, and make data-driven recommendations and decisions. This role often requires a deep understanding of machine learning, neural networks, and related technologies.
  - **Area of Specialization:** Artificial intelligence
- **Blockchain Engineer**
  - **Role Description:** Develops and implements digital solutions using blockchain technology. This role is critical in designing blockchain protocols, crafting the architecture of blockchain systems, and developing smart contracts and web apps using blockchain technology.
  - **Area of Specialization:** Blockchain technology

Enterprise Sales

- **Solutions Architect**
  - **Role Description:** Designs and orchestrates the implementation of architecture solutions that meet the specific business needs of an organization. This role involves recommending and managing hardware, software, and networks to create complete, integrated solutions.

- **Area of Specialization:** Architecture design and IT solution selling (pre-sales)
- **Systems Engineer**
  - **Role Description:** Focuses on the design, integration, and management of complex systems over their life cycles. Ensures that system performance and requirements are met, balancing the needs of business with technical feasibility.
  - **Area of Specialization:** Systems design (IT solutions)

CHAPTER SUMMARY, EXERCISES, AND CONCLUSION

Summary

The field of information technology offers a diverse array of career paths, each with its own set of challenges, opportunities, and rewards. Whether you're drawn to coding, managing networks, or leading tech projects, the key is starting with a solid foundation—just like mastering math fundamentals before tackling algebra. In IT, that foundation is networking.

Every specialization, from cloud computing to cybersecurity, builds on networking skills. By mastering the basics, you unlock doors to high-paying roles and long-term career growth. In this chapter, we broke down the key IT roles across different areas like software development, network administration, cybersecurity, and cloud computing. We also touched on some emerging roles, including AI and blockchain. Success in these fields comes from smart planning, continuous learning, and knowing when to seek help or mentorship along the way.

The journey may not always follow a straight line, but with the right blueprint, every step moves you closer to building your dream career.

Overview of IT Career Pathways

The IT industry offers a wide range of career paths, each with its own unique set of skills and opportunities. Whether you're interested in network administration, cybersecurity, cloud computing, or IT leadership, building a strong foundation is essential. Each path requires both technical expertise and soft skills to thrive.

Here are some key areas to focus on as you explore different career pathways:

- **Technical Skills:** Every role demands specific technical knowledge. For example, network engineers need to understand switching, routing, and protocols, while cybersecurity analysts must master threat detection and security tools. No matter which path you pursue, technical proficiency will be key to your success.
- **Soft Skills:** Success in IT is not just about what you know but also how you communicate and collaborate. Critical thinking, problem-solving, and project management are essential skills, especially as IT professionals frequently work across teams and need to convey technical ideas clearly to nontechnical colleagues.
- **Certifications and Degrees:** Certifications prove your ability to apply skills in real-world scenarios and are often more valued than degrees alone. If you're pursuing a career in cloud computing, consider AWS or Microsoft Azure certifications. For network professionals, CCNA or CompTIA Network+ are strong starting points. Certifications not only boost your résumé but also signal your commitment to continuous learning.

With the right combination of technical and soft skills, supported by certifications, you'll be well prepared to step into your first IT role and continue growing throughout your career.

Navigating Your IT Career Pathway

The path to success in IT isn't always linear. Whether you're starting in an entry-level help desk role, looking to move into cybersecurity, or aiming for an executive position, it's important to have a plan and be ready to adapt along the way.

Here's how you can build and navigate your IT career:

- **Entry-Level Strategies:** Focus on securing internships, leveraging networking opportunities, and obtaining entry-level certifications to enhance your job prospects.
- **Career Advancement:** Once you've built a solid foundation, pursue specialized certifications and consider advanced roles like cloud engineer or cybersecurity analyst. Continuous learning is key—technology evolves fast, and staying relevant requires commitment. Look for mentorship opportunities and leadership training to keep moving up the ladder.
- **Transitioning Between Pathways:** Switching IT career paths is common and often opens new opportunities. If you're pivoting from network engineering to cloud computing, leverage your knowledge of infrastructure while learning new tools like AWS. Identify transferable skills—such as troubleshooting or system design—that apply to multiple roles. Engage with professionals in the new field and consider shadowing or consulting to ease the transition.

Exercises

Career Mapping Exercise

Objective: Plan your career path by identifying intermediate roles and the steps required to reach your goal.

Instructions:

1. Choose a target IT role (e.g., cloud architect, cybersecurity analyst).
2. Identify three stepping-stone roles leading to that target role (e.g., IT Support → Network Engineer → Cloud Architect).
3. Map out each transition:
   - What certifications or skills are needed?
   - How long do you expect it to take?
4. Create checkpoints every 6 months to assess progress and adjust the plan.
   Bonus Tip:
   Use LinkedIn or networking events to interview professionals currently in your target role for insights on their journey.

Interview Simulations

Objective: Develop confidence by practicing for real interviews through role-play and feedback sessions.

Instructions:

1. Write down 10 common technical and behavioral questions for your target role (e.g., "Tell me about a time you handled a major IT incident").
2. Practice responses with a friend or mentor, focusing on:
   - Clear articulation of technical skills.
   - Demonstrating how you solve problems.
3. Record a session using Zoom or your phone and play it back, identifying areas to improve.
4. Refine responses over time by noting challenging questions and rehearsing answers until you're comfortable.

Reverse-Engineer Job Descriptions

Objective: Align your learning and development with real-world job market demands.

Instructions:

1. Select 3 job descriptions for your ideal IT role from platforms like LinkedIn or Indeed.
2. Highlight the skills, certifications, and experience most frequently mentioned.
3. Compare the required skills with what you currently have.
4. Assign a timeline for acquiring each.

Conclusion

Choosing your career pathway is not just about the money; it's about finding your passion. And don't worry—you don't need to have it all figured out from the get-go. What's important is having a genuine love for technology and knowing that you want to forge a career in this field. As you dive into your first networking, cybersecurity, or engineering position and become part of an IT team, you'll discover what truly captivates you.

For me, it was infrastructure. I began with help desk/server administration, which is essentially the first-line support, and rapidly realized, "Oh heck no! The help desk isn't for me." I transitioned away from that within 6 months, and honestly, I can't emphasize enough the importance of not getting stuck at the help desk. It baffles me how some people remain in this position for decades. It's essential to recognize that the help desk is merely a stepping stone, one that you don't even need if you do it right.

Bypassing the help desk is achievable through the right training, hands-on experience, and certifications. This allows you to start in an administrative or junior engineering role. And here's the thing—you can remain on the engineering path and earn even more than you would in a management role.

There's another huge misconception—that you have to go into management to climb the career ladder. That's not the case. You can progress through engineering levels one, two, three, four, and even reach the esteemed rank of a seasoned engineer at a major company like Cisco, Google, or Samsung, earning salaries of $200,000, $300,000, and even $400,000. Alternatively, you could venture into a sales engineering role, which includes titles like systems engineer, solution architect, and solution engineer.

The route I took with Cisco and Arista Networks was architecting and designing IT solutions for clients. Prior to that, I wore multiple hats, including network engineer, senior lead network engineer, and network operations center (NOC) manager, all while earning six figures.

There's also the management trajectory if you feel like that suits your personality. After gaining some experience as an engineer, you might find leadership appealing. You could oversee a team and eventually assume the role of a networking manager or IT director, supervising various groups such as storage, DevOps, networking, or help desk teams.

The hierarchy usually progresses from manager to director, then VP, and finally to the executive suite. As you continue to climb in the ranks, you could even become a CIO for a prominent company or take the entrepreneurial route and establish your own IT business.

The possibilities are boundless. Starting in an entry-level position with a salary ranging from around $60,000 to $80,000, you can quickly break into six figures. Within a decade, you could be earning anywhere from a quarter of a million to over a million dollars if you opt for business ownership, starting your own IT consulting company, or even your own tech start-up! Which reminds me of a story I want to tell you . . .. When I was working for Cisco Systems as a systems engineer, I heard about another systems engineer who founded a tech company called AppDynamics in 2008 and later sold it to Cisco Systems for $3.7 billion. This gave me the courage and inspiration to move to Silicon Valley and pursue building an educational technology–enabled platform that can train IT engineers in months rather than 4 years of college. This is one of many stories of how NGT Academy was born.

There are so many incredible pathways your career can take, and that's the allure of stepping into the realm of information technology. Keep your mindset and habits locked in and an unending number of doors will swing open for you. *Dream big!*

CHAPTER EIGHT

FIVE STEPS TO GO FROM ZERO TO ENGINEER

"Whether you think you can, or you think you can't—you're right."

— Henry Ford

INTRODUCTION

In this chapter, I'm going to give you five steps to go from Zero to Engineer, allowing you to demand six-figure job offers from Fortune 500 companies. While this is a jam-packed chapter, I'm going to show you how each of these valuable steps will save you tons of time, money, and energy that you don't want to waste. This is everything I've learned in over 25 years of being in IT, and I'm giving it to you here on a silver platter.

Are you excited? Here we go!

Step 1: Skip the help desk and do not go after the CompTIA A+ certification. A lot of people make the rookie mistake and think, "Oh, I have to start off on the help desk and then go after that A+." This is a huge mistake, and it's the first one many people make.

Too many people go to college for 4 years, get the A+, and then begin work at the help desk. Whenever I hear that pathway, I think, "Okay, so you just wasted at least $80,000 on a bachelor's degree to just go work on a help desk, paying you $10 to $15 an hour." Not only is that a waste of money, it's also a waste of time—time you can never get back. If you put the A+ certification on your résumé and accept a help desk position, sometimes you can get stuck there for years.

I have seen students work the help desk for 10-plus years because they get comfortable and complacent. Many don't feel confident that they can move into an engineer position. Trust me; you do not want to make this mistake. What you need to do instead is covered in Step 2.

Step 2: Build a rock-solid foundation by focusing on networking, and then learn network fundamentals and architecture. If you're eager to know the workings of a PC, you don't need the A+ certification. Just simply build your own PC. Yes, it's that easy. By immersing yourself in the process of assembling a PC, you'll pick up everything you need to know along the way.

This hands-on experience is invaluable because, again, you do not want to be stuck at the help desk. Setting your sights on the CompTIA Network+ or Cisco CCNA certification is a great strategy for making inroads into the IT industry. This certification is the key to bypassing the help desk, which pays below $50,000 in the United States.

By pivoting into a networking or junior engineer role, you could earn anywhere between $60,000 and $90,000 right off the bat. For example, if you are interested in architecting, deploying, and securing IT infrastructures, networking may be a path for you where you can start off as a network admin or junior network engineer.

This is one of many pathway examples—you may want to become a cybersecurity penetration tester or a software engineer. Many different career pathways will emerge for you, but networking has to be your foundation.

Remember, it's like laying the foundation for a mansion. The sturdier and more robust your networking foundation, the bigger your house can be. You have the option to either remain in networking or explore different avenues. Since networking is the foundation of the IT infrastructure, it's here to stay and the best place to start learning.

The Internet of Things (IoT) is on an explosive trajectory, with projections indicating that by 2030 there will be 50 billion devices connected to networks. These devices are what lead to network design, configuration, implementation, maintenance, and security. The network engineer's role is always in demand, and you will be responsible for managing the entire network.

Cultivating a rock-solid foundation in networking is pivotal whether your interest lies in network security, data center technologies, cloud computing, cybersecurity, automation, DevOps, or software engineering. It all traces back to networking as the bedrock.

That's Step 2—the most streamlined route into the IT ecosystem is to begin in networking. So, obtain the Network+ certification and get your foot in the door with a network position.

Step 3: Stack on multiple IT certifications. After securing your Network+ certification, the next step depends on the direction you wish to take. Let's say networking is what you most enjoy, and you want to be a network engineer; you should then pursue the Cisco CCNA certification, which can land you a six-figure engineering position.

Now, you've got both the Network+ and Cisco CCNA under your belt. I'd recommend adding perhaps even more, like the Cisco Professional Certifications. However, if you want to diversify and venture into a different technology stack, consider another certification that will help you specialize in that area. For instance, you might want to be a network engineer who transitions into a DevOps role, managing networks in the cloud for Amazon. Then you would go after some cloud certifications.

In that case, aim for the Amazon certification, and stack that alongside your Network+ and CCNA. That's just one example. But what if your goal is to become a network security engineer? In this instance, you could stack your Network+ and CCNA, and then pursue the Security+, and if your interest lies in defending networks from malicious actors as part of the blue team, you might want to go for the EC-Council Network Defense Essentials certification. If you want pursue cloud technologies, then you would get the Amazon AWS Cloud certification. Ultimately, it hinges on the role you're vying for and what your dream IT job looks like.

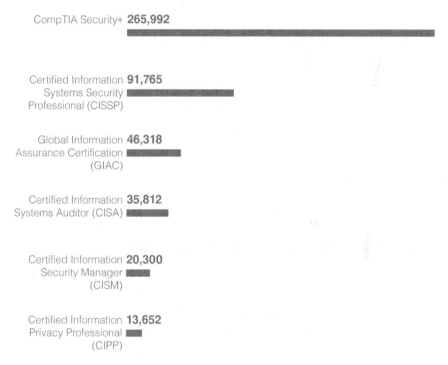

CompTIA Security+ **265,992**

Certified Information **91,765**
Systems Security
Professional (CISSP)

Global Information **46,318**
Assurance Certification
(GIAC)

Certified Information **35,812**
Systems Auditor (CISA)

Certified Information **20,300**
Security Manager
(CISM)

Certified Information **13,652**
Privacy Professional
(CIPP)

Now, the real trick to propelling and accelerating your pay scale is to tirelessly continue amassing these certifications. Save yourself time and concentrate your energy on certifications. When you have six, nine, or even 12 certifications to your name, your résumé will be sizzling. You'll be a hot commodity for employers, and you'll find yourself swimming in job offers, sometimes on a weekly basis, just by having a polished LinkedIn profile.

Certified Information Systems Security Professional (CISSP) **97,555**

CompTIA Security+ **86,066**

Certified Information Systems Auditor (CISA) **75,040**

Global Information Assurance Certification (GIAC) **52,807**

Certified Information Security Manager (CISM) **49,519**

Certified Information Privacy Professional (CIPP) **8,797**

And this leads us to Step 4, which goes hand in hand with Step 3 . . .

Step 4: Work on IT projects inside your department. The best way to grasp the breadth of projects in the IT ecosystem is to schedule a meeting with your manager or the department head, such as your VP, IT director, or even the CIO, and ask about the current projects. Also, if you're relatively new to the company, don't hesitate to volunteer.

It's essential that you focus on immersing yourself in IT projects, actively participating and eventually taking the reins on your own IT project. You see, every IT department has an allocated budget for the calendar year, and within this budget lies the IT projects. Why is this relevant? Because this is the breeding ground for innovation. This is where IT solutions are crafted to address business challenges. When you play a role in making an impact within the organization, your stock rises. Then, of course, your salary follows suit. Plus, while you're working on these projects, you have the opportunity to stack on additional certifications.

For instance, if I'm deep in a phone system upgrade, transitioning from a traditional PBX telephone setup to cutting-edge digital voice over IP, I might set my sights on a voice certification and make it a part of the project. It's a savvy way to juggle two objectives simultaneously and level up. The more projects you notch on your belt, the faster you'll find your career on an upward trajectory. Doing this is how you acquire a wealth of skills that can demand a six-figure salary.

Step 5: Secure the engineer job title ASAP.   Once you are able to work on multiple IT projects, you want to start thinking about how to secure the engineer job title. By this point, maybe you're a network admin, a technician, or an analyst. Getting the engineer job title will only advance and increase your income because employers pay by the industry-standard salary scales.

An engineer is always going to get paid more than an administrator or a technician. Once you secure the engineer job title, you can start leading projects. That's what you most want to do because building a portfolio is important to do early on in your career. Steps 4 and 5 were the reasons I was able to go from making $28,000 to breaking six figures in less than two years!

Securing the engineer job title is a huge achievement, but it just marks the first part of what you're capable of. Once you achieve that goal, you will want to become the team lead or the point person when it comes to running new IT projects. This is key. In the next chapter, you will learn what propelled me to go from a low six-figure income to a high six-figure income, getting job offers anywhere from $200,000 to $350,000.

CHAPTER SUMMARY, EXERCISES, AND CONCLUSION

Summary

Transitioning from an aspiring IT professional to a skilled engineer requires strategic planning, dedication, and the right approach. This chapter provides a five-step framework to fast-track your progress and avoid the pitfalls that often slow people down. The journey focuses on building a solid foundation, gaining specialized knowledge, acquiring hands-on experience, expanding your professional network, and committing to continuous learning.

Step 1: Establish a Strong Foundation

Start by mastering the essentials of networking, hardware, and security principles. This foundation supports everything you'll learn moving forward. Skip irrelevant certifications like A+ and instead aim for networking certifications, such as Network+ or CCNA.

Step 2: Gain Specialized Knowledge

Once you have a solid foundation, the next step is to specialize in a specific area of IT that aligns with your career goals. This specialization will help you stand out in the job market.

- **Selecting a Specialty:** Choose a focus area such as network engineering, cybersecurity, or cloud computing based on your interests and market demand.
- **Advanced Training:** Enroll in advanced courses and earn certifications specific to your chosen specialty. Certifications such as CCNA

for networking or AWS Certified Solutions Architect for cloud computing can be highly beneficial.

- **Practical Projects:** Engage in projects that allow you to apply what you've learned in real-world scenarios. This could be contributing to open source projects, developing your own software, or setting up network configurations in a simulated environment.

Step 3: Acquire Hands-On Experience

Practical experience is crucial for understanding real-world applications and proving your capabilities to potential employers.

- **Internships and Apprenticeships:** Look for internship opportunities that provide hands-on experience in your area of specialization. Even unpaid internships can be valuable for gaining practical experience.
- **Freelance Projects:** Take on freelance projects to build a portfolio of work that you can showcase to potential employers. Platforms like Upwork or Freelancer can be good places to start.
- **Volunteer Work:** Offer your IT skills to nonprofits or local organizations. This not only helps you gain experience but also expands your professional network.

Step 4: Build Your Professional Network

Networking is essential in the IT industry. Building relationships with other IT professionals can lead to job opportunities, mentorship, and collaborative projects.

- **Attend Industry Conferences and Meetups:** Participate in IT-related events in your area or online. Events like tech meetups, seminars, and conferences are great for meeting people and learning about new technologies and trends.

- **Join Professional Organizations:** Become a member of professional IT organizations such as the Institute of Electrical and Electronics Engineers (IEEE), the Association for Computing Machinery (ACM), or ISACA. These organizations offer networking opportunities, resources, and professional development activities.
- **Utilize Social Media:** Engage with the IT community on platforms like LinkedIn, X, and GitHub. Share your projects, contribute to discussions, and connect with industry leaders.

Step 5: Commit to Continuous Learning

The IT field is constantly evolving, making continuous learning essential to maintain your relevance and competitiveness in the industry.

- **Stay Updated with Industry Trends:** Follow industry news, subscribe to tech blogs, and participate in webinars and workshops to keep up with new technologies and methodologies.
- **Ongoing Education:** Continue to take courses and earn new certifications even after securing a job. This commitment to learning will help you advance in your career and adapt to changes in technology.
- **Peer Learning Groups:** Join or form study groups with peers who are also interested in staying current with IT advancements. These groups can provide support, motivation, and insights as you continue to grow professionally.

Exercises

Use these exercises to apply what you've learned in this chapter and build momentum in your IT career journey.

Set Yearly Certification Goals

Objective: Strategically build expertise and stay relevant by earning certifications aligned with your career path and industry trends.

Instructions:

1. **Select Target Certifications:**
   - Identify one primary certification relevant to your current role or career goal.
   - Explore additional complementary skills or niche certifications to stay competitive (e.g., cloud, security, AI).
2. **Create a Preparation Plan:**
   - Map out milestones (e.g., complete modules by Month 2, practice tests by Month 4).
   - Allocate weekly study blocks (e.g., 1 hour/day or 5 hours/week). Use platforms like Trello or Notion to track your progress.

Enhanced Project Portfolio Development

Objective: Build a hands-on project that demonstrates your technical abilities and problem-solving skills.

Instructions:

1. Select a challenging project relevant to your field.
   - Example: Configure and monitor a network using Cisco Packet Tracer.
   - Example: Deploy a web application using cloud services like AWS or Azure.
2. Document the project life cycle, including the problem statement, your approach, troubleshooting steps, and the final solution.

3. Create a public repository on GitHub or build a simple portfolio website to showcase your work.

4. Include reflections about what you learned and how you overcame challenges, making this resource interview-ready.

Skill Exchange Partnerships

Objective: Collaborate with others to exchange knowledge and build expertise across IT domains.

Instructions:

1. Identify two professionals or peers with complementary skills (e.g., one expert in networking, the other in cloud computing).

2. Set up biweekly knowledge exchange sessions where each person teaches a new concept or walks through a project they're working on.

3. Keep shared notes to track what you learn and identify areas for deeper exploration.

4. Use this partnership to build accountability and grow your understanding across multiple IT pathways.

Expand Your Industry Presence with Intentional Involvement

Objective: Stay relevant in the tech space by actively engaging with industry professionals and participating in networking events.

Instructions:

1. **Commit to Major Tech Events:**
   - Attend at least two key conferences (in person or virtually) that align with your career interests, such as AWS, Cisco Live, or Black Hat.

2. **Engage Between Major Events:**
   - Between larger events, participate in local meetups, webinars, or online communities (like GitHub, Slack groups, or tech forums) at least once a month.
   - Platforms such as Meetup.com or Eventbrite can help you discover relevant opportunities.

3. **Document Takeaways and Connections:**
   - After every event or meeting, document key takeaways—whether it's a new trend, a skill to learn, or someone to follow up with.
   - Maintain a networking log where you track who you met, what you discussed, and when to follow up. This ensures you remain active and intentional in expanding your professional network.

4. **Turn Connections into Collaborations:**
   - Use these events to create meaningful relationships, such as finding mentors, collaborators, or job referrals. Apply what you learn by integrating new trends into your work or projects.

Conclusion

Following these five steps can significantly streamline your journey from an aspiring IT professional to a skilled engineer. By establishing a strong foundation, gaining specialized knowledge, acquiring practical experience, building a professional network, and committing to continuous learning, you can enhance your career prospects and achieve your professional goals in the IT industry.

CHAPTER NINE

FOUR MORE STEPS TO DEMAND SIX-FIGURE JOB OFFERS FROM FORTUNE 500 COMPANIES

"Work hard in silence, let your success be the noise."
— Frank Ocean

INTRODUCTION

While you may not yet be an engineer, use these next four steps to set your sights on the life you may have never dreamed was possible. Do it right now. I dare you. Envision yourself as a tech CEO, an IT executive, or a highly specialized contractor making over $1 million every single year.

That's all well within reach, if and only if you follow Steps 1 through 9. (You already saw Steps 1–5 in Chapter 8, "Five Steps to Go from Zero to Engineer.") If I can do it and lead others to it, you can do it too. All you have to do is see yourself and remember to *feel* yourself living that life. What does it look like? What do you see? What kind of activities are you doing? How do you treat people? How do people treat you? Really immerse yourself into that world. And now, read the four more steps that will help you demand six-figure job offers from Fortune 500 companies!

Step 6: Surround yourself with smarter engineers. Here's how . . .
When you're a part of the IT team, shadow the brightest engineers within your department and absorb knowledge from them. Additionally, you can gain insights from those who enter your organization to pitch IT solutions. For instance, when you're immersed in Step 4, working on those projects, you'll want to observe who's involved in them.

There's often a team lead within your IT department spearheading the project, and they'll bring in vendors. So, think about the entire IT ecosystem. You have manufacturers like Cisco, Dell, AWS, or Palo Alto Networks, who are eager to sell you their software and hardware technology. Well, they're going to send over their best engineers to pitch their products.

They'll also introduce engineers and account managers from the channel partner side. Therefore, you want to get involved with these consultants. There might even be a consultant specifically brought in to oversee that project, and you'll want to shadow them. Consider them your mentors. You don't even need to formally ask them, "Will you be my mentor?" Just simply inquire, engage in discussions, shadow them, and immerse yourself in these projects.

You've may have heard the adage, "Your net worth is the average of the five people you spend the most time with." The same principle applies to evolving into a high-earning IT professional—surround yourself with individuals who are not only smarter but also earn more than you.

Why? Because this environment is going to naturally elevate you. This is a vital step because often individuals are held back by their egos and pride, and they aspire to always be the most intelligent person in the room. This fixed mindset won't serve you well, especially in the early stages of your career. By following these steps, and taking care of your mindset, you might be the most knowledgeable person in the room. But that's for other people to say to you, not something for you to waste time trying to convince others.

At all stages, it's crucial to maintain connections with peers and colleagues who can challenge and inspire you to ascend to new heights. It's always about leveling up, unveiling your inner greatness, and morphing into the best version of yourself while never ceasing to grow. And that leads us right into Step 7.

Step 7: Specialize and become a subject matter expert (SME)—aka picking up on trends. At this stage of your career, you're probably 3 to 5 years in, and this is when you want to specialize in a specific technology and become a subject matter expert (SME). One effective approach to accomplishing this is to latch onto emerging trends. Why? Because if you can tap into a trend in its infancy, within 3 to 5 years, you'll likely be recognized as an SME and a thought leader in that area, just because you had the foresight to embrace it early on.

In 2005, when I was working at a credit union as a network technician and progressing to become a network engineer, I volunteered to lead a project focused on an old PBX phone system on the brink of dying out. At that time, voiceover IP was gaining momentum; everyone was making the switch from analog to digital. This innovation infiltrated networking, bringing with it an increasing need for voice, video, and data network convergence.

The voice and video trend was monumental. When I jumped on that trend, I got high-demand skills that were fresh in the market. Securing my Cisco Certified Voice Professional certification and being recognized as an SME was a direct result of this. Trends like these surface regularly. We've seen the rise of voice and video, then cloud technologies, and currently, the explosion of AI automation, DevOps, and various IT domains.

Capitalizing on these trends and specializing in them will massively propel your career and income. You'll find yourself in high demand, and this alone can help you double your income.

Step 8: Work on either getting promoted or growing out of the company. Becoming an SME can help you get promoted within your current company, possibly even leading to the creation of a new job title tailored to your expertise. Let me share an example. We had a substantial network security and firewall upgrade project that needed handling, and I dove into that technology, learning and specializing in it. This led to me becoming a network security engineer specializing in firewall intrusion detection, intrusion prevention, and malware detection. This specialization opened up a world of opportunities for me in the cybersecurity domain.

You can replicate this success across any new IT trend or technology. If you're an early adopter, think about where you'll stand in the marketplace years down the road. You'll likely find yourself in the top 5 percent, having spent the longest time learning and mastering it. This is one of the crucial ways to break into the highest levels of the IT industry.

Also, avoid fixating on promotion within your current job. If they're unwilling to provide what you deserve, be ready to develop an exit strategy. In the past, it was seen as unwise if you didn't stick with a company for several years. However, these days it's commonplace to move on after a year or two. Still, I suggest staying at a company for about 2–5 years, assuming they're treating you well.

Be prepared to part ways if the company isn't looking out for your best interests. It's vital to take full responsibility for accelerating and advancing your career without wasting time.

Ten Strategies for Getting Promoted Quickly

Strategy 1: Bring positive emotions into your work environment. No manager wants someone around who's complaining or whining all the time. So, bring a positive attitude; that's first.

Strategy 2: Show up to work early. If you want to get that promotion, you have to stand out from the pack. I suggest showing up 15 minutes early and leaving 15 minutes late.

Be the first one in the office and the last one out. Any good manager will notice that.

Strategy 3: Journal your work. This is an important step because if you don't journal your work, you'll fail to fully understand the projects you're working on, what milestones you've accomplished, and what value and impact you've made. No one's going to do that for you. The real secret here is to take that journal to your work every week, every month, and every quarter.

You can then roll that into an executive summary **(Strategy 4)** of two or more pages that you can use in your biannual or yearly performance review. This is key in getting promoted because now you have proof about what you've done. Most likely, none of your peers have done this (unless they've read this book!). So when it comes to that open engineer position, you're going to be top of the list because you're basically making it a no-brainer for your manager to choose you.

Strategy 5: Always be a team player. Managers want to see that you can contribute to the entire department and provide value. Volunteer when opportunities arise. Be the first one to raise your hand or help others—and help out with a humble heart. That's being a team player.

Strategy 6: Take the lead on a project or project(s). Step 4 advises working on projects, but now, you want to be *leading* projects. That's going to put you in the spotlight. Don't be afraid to take on more responsibility because doing so pushes you out of your comfort zone. That's an opportunity for you to learn new skills and technologies that will help further advance your career.

That's how I was able to go from a support technician to a network engineer: because I took on extra responsibilities. I justified a job title change with my VP of IT and the HR manager. Here's a tip: Every year, IT departments budget for IT expenditures and projects. By volunteering for this budgeting task, you can help out the department, and if you're able to do that, you'll stand out from the pack.

Strategy 7: Set your sights on a company award, such as Employee of the Year. Once I got Employee of the Year by working on multiple projects, and I was able to use that to help justify my promotion.

Strategy 8: Ask HR to provide your job description, if you don't have one already. Review the listed duties and responsibilities carefully, and identify tasks that fall outside the scope of your current role. These are opportunities to take on additional responsibilities and work on more complex projects.

As you expand your contributions beyond your original role, you can start drafting a new job description—and even propose a new title—that reflects the extra value you bring to the company. This proactive approach not only positions you for promotions but also makes you indispensable to the organization.

Strategy 9: Research salary details and know what the market is paying for any of the positions that you're aiming for. Using sites like http://salary.com will help you pull off your pay raise request with confidence and ease.

Strategy 10: Set up a quarterly or biannual review with your manager if you don't already do so. I recommend a review every quarter because, that way, you can plant seeds and build rapport with your manager. This will increase understanding as you communicate how much you're growing and providing value to the department. One year later, when you ask for that promotion or whenever an open position comes up and you apply, you're going to be at the top of the radar and it's a done deal.

Step 9: Join the major leagues or start your own consulting company. What I mean by joining the major leagues is working with the manufacturers. Entering the minor leagues involves joining value-added resellers (VARs) or a managed service provider (MSP) that resells the OEM manufacturer technology solutions. These partners essentially resell through Cisco's channel. This is how Cisco goes to market with its products. So, joining a VAR is the minor leagues, and sometimes that's a necessary step before making it to the major leagues.

With a stroke of luck, you might bypass the minors and land directly in the majors, like I did. I transitioned from working at a credit union as a senior network engineer to being scouted and recruited by Cisco Systems. To do what I did, you have to be at the top of your game. It takes years of dedication to join where the top 10 percent of IT professionals work. These tech giants are at the forefront of cutting-edge technology.

Getting into the major leagues is what I recommend as soon as you can. Even just starting at an entry-level technical assistance center, or becoming a Cisco support engineer, you can climb the ladder to become a systems consulting engineer.

Being part of the major leagues comes with major perks. First, you can demand the highest salary in the market. You'll also have access to company stock options and grants at huge discounts, and sometimes even receive a sign-up bonus that could range anywhere from $15,000 to $25,000!

On top of that, you might qualify for bonuses and commissions, as I did at Cisco Systems. This enabled me to receive $10,000+ biweekly paychecks through a combination of a six-figure base salary, bonuses, and commissions, not to mention my stock options. As a solution engineer, architect, or systems engineer in the major leagues, you could rake in anywhere from $200,000 to $400,000, inclusive of all the perks—obviously worth the time, hard work, and following all nine of these steps!

If you dream of working for a large Fortune 100 company, that's also joining the major leagues. While the pay might be slightly less, it varies. As an architect at a Fortune 100 company, you might still clear over $200,000. Whatever pathway you choose, these careers are key before transitioning to become your own IT consultant or launching your IT firm. That's where you make more money than you've ever imagined possible.

By stepping into the major leagues, you're almost guaranteed to make a high six-figure salary compared to a low six-figure one. So that's Step 9. I wish someone had clued me in on this when I began my career because I was oblivious to what I call "the other side of the table." My perception was that the IT team only existed on the customer side. It wasn't until I accidentally stumbled upon the other side of the table when working on my voiceover IP project at the credit union. I immediately realized the potential.

A senior systems engineer from one of the channel partners came in, and I shadowed him. As I said, it's important to surround yourself with more knowledgeable and experienced engineers. After building rapport as the lead point of contact for the IT project, it dawned on me that while I was making a low six-figure salary, he was earning double, simply because he was part of the other side of the table working on major league projects.

"Dreams don't work unless you do."

— *John C. Maxwell*

Generally, around five to seven years into your career, you can make the leap into the major leagues. With this step, just like me, you'll be breaking into higher salary brackets that you could never have dreamed of or even knew existed.

CHAPTER SUMMARY, EXERCISES, AND CONCLUSION

Summary

Securing a six-figure job offer from a top-tier company is a dream for many IT professionals. This chapter unveiled four critical steps that can dramatically increase your chances of landing these coveted positions. We explored how to make yourself indispensable in the job market, leverage your network effectively, and master the art of negotiation.

Step 1: Become an Expert in High-Demand Skills

To command a six-figure salary, you need to offer skills that are in high demand and short supply. This means staying ahead of the curve in rapidly evolving IT fields such as cybersecurity, cloud computing, and data science.

- **Identify High-Demand Skills:** Research current trends in the IT job market to identify which skills are most sought after by top companies. Resources like industry reports, job postings, and professional forums can provide valuable insights.
- **Continuous Learning and Certification:** Obtain certifications that validate your expertise in these areas. Certifications from

recognized bodies like CompTIA, Cisco, AWS, and Microsoft not only enhance your résumé, but also signal your commitment to professional growth.

- **Specialize in Niche Areas:** Consider specializing in niche areas within broader fields. For example, in cybersecurity, you might focus on ethical hacking or compliance. This specialization can make you particularly valuable to employers looking for experts in specific areas.

Step 2: Build a Robust Professional Network

Networking is often the bridge between being a qualified candidate and becoming a sought-after professional. Building strong relationships within the industry can lead to insider knowledge on job openings and personal endorsements that can be crucial during the hiring process.

- **Attend Industry Events:** Regularly attend conferences, seminars, and workshops. These are not only great for learning but also for meeting influential people in your field.
- **Engage on Professional Platforms:** Actively participate in discussions on platforms like LinkedIn. Share insights, comment on posts, and publish articles relevant to your expertise.
- **Develop Meaningful Relationships:** Don't just network for the sake of it. Focus on building meaningful relationships where you can offer value. This could involve helping others, sharing opportunities, or collaborating on projects.

Step 3: Master the Art of Negotiation

Knowing how to negotiate effectively can be the difference between a standard job offer and a six-figure salary. Understanding your worth and being able to articulate it confidently is key.

- **Research Market Salaries:** Use tools like Glassdoor, PayScale, and industry salary surveys to understand what companies are willing to pay for someone with your qualifications and experience in your region.

- **Articulate Your Value:** Prepare to clearly explain how your skills and experiences will benefit the potential employer. Be ready to discuss specific examples of how you have positively impacted previous organizations.
- **Negotiation Tactics:** Learn negotiation tactics to use when discussing job offers. Know when to push for more and when to compromise. Practicing negotiations with a mentor or coach can be highly beneficial.

Exercises

These exercises are designed to solidify your learning and build momentum toward achieving six-figure job offers:

Shadow and Learn

- Identify 2–3 engineers or consultants in your company or network who work on advanced IT projects.
- Schedule time to shadow them during key meetings or projects.
- Write down three new skills or tools you learn from each experience and reflect on how you can apply them in your role.
  - Example: Observed cloud architecture discussions with AWS engineers and learned about multiregion deployment strategies.

Identify and Track Industry Trends

- Research emerging trends in IT, such as AI, automation, or DevOps.
- Select one trend and create a learning plan to specialize in it.
  - Example: Study AI automation tools and complete relevant certifications or projects over the next 6 months.

- Track the trend's development, attend webinars or events related to it, and engage with industry thought leaders on LinkedIn or X.

Draft Your Next Job Title

- Review your current job description and identify tasks you've taken on that go beyond the role's scope.
- Write a new job title and description that reflects these responsibilities.
  - Example: Network Security Engineer specializing in firewall intrusion prevention and detection.
- Schedule a conversation with your manager to propose the updated title and discuss your future career path.

Set Quarterly Growth Objectives

Every quarter, select one major goal to work toward:

- Q1: Earn CCNA certification.
- Q2: Shadow senior engineers on at least two IT projects.
- Q3: Present a project you led in your department to leadership.

Create a Career Trend Road Map

- Choose a technology trend (e.g., AI, DevOps, cloud) and develop a 1-to-3-year plan to become an expert in that area.
- Include specific certifications, projects, and networking opportunities to pursue.
  - Example: Complete AWS Solutions Architect certification in Year 1, work on a cloud migration project in Year 2, and present at a cloud conference in Year 3.

Track Your Value with a Performance Journal

- Maintain a weekly or monthly journal where you log your accomplishments, milestones, and contributions to IT projects.

- Use this journal to build an executive summary every quarter and discuss it during performance reviews with your manager.
  - Example: Implemented a firewall upgrade that reduced downtime by 25%.

Conclusion

Landing a six-figure job offer in the IT industry is achievable by becoming highly skilled in valuable areas, building a robust professional network, and mastering negotiation techniques. This chapter provided you with practical strategies, exercises, and an action plan to enhance your attractiveness to Fortune 500 companies, helping you to not only reach but exceed your career goals.

CHAPTER TEN

BRIDGING THE "GAP"

"If you can't yet do great things, do small things in a great way."
— Napoleon Hill

S o, what is the "gap?" The gap refers to the space between where we are and where we want to be. Gap analysis measures the difference between the expected performance in an organization, in a business, or in a personal endeavor and the actual process to get there. It can also be called a need analysis, need assessment, or need-gap analysis. Basically, to get where you want to be, it's not a straight line. We often think that by clearly defining our goal, it's a direct route from here to there. The reality is not quite so simple, nor should it be.

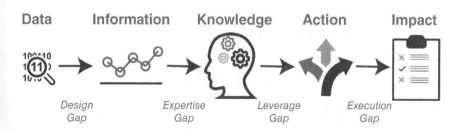

Data	Information	Knowledge	Action	Impact
Design Gap	Expertise Gap	Leverage Gap	Execution Gap	

Understanding the "gap" is crucial in any transformation journey, especially in transitioning from a novice to an expert in the IT field. The gap represents the distance between your current position and where you aspire to be—becoming an engineer. Often, this journey is visualized as a straightforward path, but in reality, it's more complex and filled with essential learning curves and decisions that shape your professional growth.

UNDERSTANDING GAP ANALYSIS

Gap analysis is defined as a strategic tool used to compare where you are with where you want to be. This analysis helps you identify areas of improvement and the actions you need to take to close the gap.

Why It Matters

In IT, where technologies and required skills evolve rapidly, understanding your current capabilities and how they match up against industry standards or job requirements is crucial.

You're likely starting out with a skill level of Zero, and your goal is to be an engineer. To get from Zero to Engineer is not a straight line. For the first few months, it looks and feels as if your skill level stays at Zero—and in many ways, it does. But this is where you have to dig in and stay focused. This is where the lessons in this book will keep you on mission even when it feels like you're not getting anywhere.

Closing the Gap

The first step to bridging the gap is to understand the distance between your current skills and the expertise required for your desired role.

- **Assessing Skills and Knowledge Gaps:** Begin with a personal skills audit—compare your current knowledge with the qualifications required for your target job. Use job descriptions or industry resources like LinkedIn and CyberSeek to identify gaps. For example, if you want to become a cloud engineer, you may realize that you need proficiency in platforms like AWS or Azure, and certifications such as AWS Solutions Architect.
- **Setting Priorities:** Not every gap needs immediate attention. Identify which skills and certifications are essential for your next role and which can wait. Focusing on high-impact areas will keep you on track and prevent overwhelm.

Once you have a clear understanding of where you are and where you need to be, the next step is creating a plan that transforms your goals into actionable steps. Break your goal into manageable milestones—such as earning a certification or completing a project. Be flexible with your timelines, but stay consistent. Use a simple tracking system to monitor your progress and adjust goals as needed.

Learning Through Action and Feedback

Real learning happens when you apply your skills in real-world scenarios. Whether it's contributing to a project at work, freelancing, or volunteering, seek out opportunities that challenge you to practice what you've learned. Document these experiences to build a portfolio that highlights your technical abilities and practical problem-solving skills.

At the same time, *feedback is essential* to growth. Regularly connect with mentors, managers, or peers who can provide insight into your progress. Whether it's formal reviews or casual check-ins, listen actively to what they say. Pay attention to both strengths and areas for improvement. Use their input to refine your approach, align your efforts with industry standards, and ensure that each new project pushes you closer to your goal. Learning is an iterative process—applying skills, gathering feedback, and adjusting your approach will help you grow faster and more effectively.

The Journey's Realities

While the goal is clear—transition from Zero to Engineer—the path is neither straight nor predictable. Initially, your progress might feel stagnant, as foundational skills and knowledge are being built quietly under the surface. The following are key phases and strategies that shape this transformative journey:

- **Early Stages:** These stages are characterized by seemingly slow progress. You're accumulating essential knowledge and skills that don't yet manifest as progress in your career.
- **Decision Points:** Choices about certifications, projects, and specific job roles are not merely checkboxes. Each decision is a strategic step toward building a robust portfolio that aligns with your career aspirations.
- **Leveraging Lessons to Propel Forward:** The initial chapters of this book are not just introductory—they are foundational. They keep you anchored to your mission, especially during periods when tangible progress feels elusive.
- **Strategic Learning:** Every chapter until now has layered on essential skills and strategic thinking necessary to navigate your journey effectively.
- **Mindset and Persistence:** Maintaining a positive and growth-oriented mindset is pivotal. The daily choices you make about how to approach challenges and opportunities will determine your trajectory.

While it feels like your skill line stays at Zero for the first few months, that line is actually filled with twists and turns. This certification or that one? This job or that one? These projects or those other ones? So many directions! But as long as you're remembering the lessons from this book, those twists will all be a critical part of your path. Remember that upward or downward spiral? This is where you get to make choices on projects, certifications, trainings, and, most of all, your mindset every single day. Do this and have faith that the path from Zero to Engineer will land you your dream job and your dream life!

The truth is that, before you know it, after enduring the first few months your rise from Zero to Engineer will happen almost overnight! This is that huge swing up you see in the graph. After making all the best decisions, keeping a focused mindset, having a grateful heart, and following your natural curiosity, you could land that engineer title in just four months. But to do that, you're going to need some help.

To make your path from Zero to Engineer be as dynamic, comprehensive, and supportive as possible, I created NGT Academy. I've referenced it throughout the book, but now, if you haven't already, it's time you signed up. NGT Academy is on a mission to help 1 million people get tech jobs by 2030. Why? Because there will be 3 million unfilled IT jobs in the market by 2025. According to All Work, this means there's an incredible 13 percent growth rate!

By taking advantage of an affordable education, you will be job-ready for a career in cybersecurity. As I've made crystal clear, college is not the answer. You shouldn't be left with outrageous debt from degrees that don't teach you the required skills to succeed in the workplace.

NGT Academy has the best program to equip anyone to be IT specialists in the fastest way possible. We do this by teaching a strong foundation in network architecture before students go into our cybersecurity training. Once you master the fundamentals of networking, you are best prepared for additional training programs along with real-world projects.

With hands-on learning combined with our proven methods, we'll give you everything you need. While you alone hold the power of what decisions you make, NGT Academy is here, and I am here, for you to mind the "gap" as you go from Zero to Engineer! The following figure shows the Ultimate IT Blueprint Pyramid, a structured representation of step-by-step skills acquisition from foundational to specialized knowledge in IT (for more, see Chapter 11).

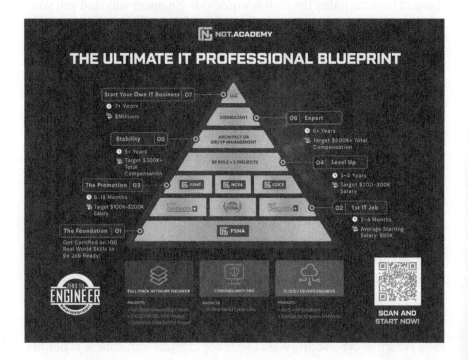

Transformation Realized

The transition may feel gradual, but with the right foundation, the shift from learning to application—and ultimately to mastery—can seem sudden and dramatic.

Once the foundational period is past, you are poised to rise quickly. The skills and knowledge acquired start to manifest as significant advancements in capability and job opportunities.

Introducing NGT Academy

To make your journey as comprehensive and supportive as possible, NGT Academy offers tailored educational pathways designed specifically for rapid, practical career development in IT.

- **Mission-Driven Education:** With the goal to fill the burgeoning demand in the IT job market, NGT Academy provides an accelerated, focused educational experience that prepares you for real-world IT roles without the burden of excessive debt.
- **Curriculum Focus:** Starting with network architecture fundamentals, the program seamlessly transitions into specialized training in cybersecurity, equipping you with a broad yet detailed skill set.
- **Hands-On Learning:** Combining theoretical knowledge with practical application ensures that you are not just learning but also applying concepts in real-world scenarios, enhancing retention and competence.

As you venture from Zero to Engineer, remember that the path is yours to shape. While NGT Academy provides the road map and tools, your decisions, persistence, and dedication to continuous learning will determine your success. Mind the gap by making informed choices, leveraging available resources, and committing to your growth every step of the way. This chapter doesn't just guide you; it empowers you to take control of your career and bridge the gap with confidence and clarity.

CHAPTER SUMMARY, EXERCISES, AND CONCLUSION

Summary

In every IT professionals career, there comes a time when you identify a gap between where you are and where you want to be. This chapter focused on identifying those gaps—be they skills, knowledge, or experience—and effectively bridging them to advance your career. We explored strategies for assessing your current situation, identifying needed improvements, and systematically addressing these areas to align closer with your career objectives.

Understanding Your Current Position

The first step in bridging any gap is understanding your current status accurately. This requires a thorough assessment of your skills, knowledge, experience, and how they compare to the requirements of your desired job or career advancement.

- **Skills Audit:** Conduct a comprehensive review of your technical and soft skills. List all the skills you possess and rate your proficiency in each area.
- **Performance Feedback:** Regularly seek feedback from peers, supervisors, and mentors to gain an external perspective on your abilities and areas that may need improvement.
- **Industry Requirements:** Stay updated on the latest trends and demands in your field. Regularly review job postings similar to your dream job to understand what employers are currently seeking.

Planning Your Development

Once you understand where the gaps lie, the next step is to create a tailored development plan to address these deficiencies effectively.

- **Setting Specific Goals:** Based on your skills audit and the requirements of your target position, set specific, measurable goals for improvement.
- **Choosing the Right Resources:** Identify the best resources to help you develop the necessary skills. This might include courses, workshops, books, or online tutorials.
- **Creating a Timeline:** Develop a realistic timeline for achieving your goals, breaking down the path to smaller milestones that can be achieved more manageably.

Implementing Your Plan

With a clear development plan in place, the focus shifts to implementation. Staying committed and tracking your progress are crucial to successfully bridging the gap.

- **Regular Learning Schedule:** Dedicate regular time slots each week for learning and development activities to ensure consistent progress.
- **Practical Application:** Look for opportunities to apply new skills in real-world scenarios, whether in your current job, through freelance projects, or in a volunteer capacity.
- **Progress Reviews:** Set up regular intervals to review your progress against your goals. Adjust your strategies as necessary to stay on track.

Overcoming Common Obstacles

During your journey, you may encounter several obstacles that can derail your progress. Addressing these proactively is key to successful development.

- **Motivation Fluctuations:** Find ways to stay motivated over the long term, such as setting up rewards for achieving milestones or partnering with a study buddy.
- **Resource Limitations:** If resources like time and money are limited, prioritize your learning activities based on which skills are most crucial for your career advancement.
- **Adapting to Change:** The IT field is rapidly evolving, and new technologies can shift the landscape. Be flexible and ready to update your development plan as the industry changes.

Exercises

Skills Gap Analysis Workshop

Objective: Conduct a thorough analysis to identify skill gaps and prioritize their importance.

Instructions:

- List your current technical and soft skills and compare them against the requirements for your desired role using job postings or professional resources.
- Categorize the gaps into high, medium, and low priority based on relevance and market demand.
- Develop a mini action plan for each high-priority gap, including specific learning resources or activities (e.g., "Enroll in a cybersecurity fundamentals course within three weeks").
- Revisit your analysis every 3–6 months to track progress and update priorities.

Development Plan Creation

Objective: Build a structured development plan to close skill gaps effectively.

Instructions:

- Based on your gap analysis, outline a development plan with clear goals and timelines for achieving each skill.
- Identify the resources required (e.g., online courses, certifications, mentorship).
- Break down each goal into milestones (e.g., "Complete first module of AWS training in one month") and monitor your progress.
- Use project management tools like Trello or Notion to organize tasks and stay consistent.

Feedback Collection System

Objective: Collect regular feedback to improve skills and track performance growth.

Instructions:

- Identify 2–3 trusted individuals (mentors, managers, peers) to provide structured feedback.
- Schedule quarterly check-ins or surveys for feedback focused on specific areas (technical skills, teamwork, communication).
- Use a template or online survey to gather input. Categorize the feedback into themes and create small, actionable steps for improvement.
- Review feedback regularly and adjust your development plan based on insights.

Annual Career Strategy Retreat

Objective: Review and realign your long-term career goals annually.

Instructions:

- Set aside a day each year to evaluate your career progress, reflect on your achievements, and identify any new challenges.

- Assess whether your current development plan aligns with market trends and your evolving career aspirations.
- Adjust your strategies and development goals to stay on track toward your desired role.
- Use this time to set new goals, outline next steps, and identify any certifications or skills to pursue in the coming year.

Conclusion

Bridging the gap between your current position and where you want to be in your IT career is a dynamic and ongoing process. By accurately assessing your skills, setting targeted goals, and methodically working toward them, you can effectively close these gaps and advance your career. This chapter provided you with the strategies, exercises, and action plan needed to systematically improve and position yourself for success in the competitive field of IT.

CHAPTER ELEVEN

THE ULTIMATE IT PROFESSIONAL BLUEPRINT

INTRODUCTION

In this chapter, I want to share my journey from earning $28,000 a year to receiving a $350,000 total comp package at a Fortune 500 company to eventually making millions by starting my own IT training and consultancy business. You already know my story, but I wanted to add this chapter to explain the pyramid structure breaking down each step and how I quickly moved up the ranks in IT using certain tactics, strategies, and insights proven to give you an edge among your peers!

This transformation was possible by following the principles and strategies outlined in this chapter through seven stages. This is the same pyramid diagram mentioned in Chapter 10, "Bridging the 'Gap,'" which represents over 20 years of working in IT compressed into a single visual. The journey wasn't easy; it required dedication, hard work, sacrifice, and learning from mistakes. I faced numerous challenges, from understanding the intricacies of IT engineering and training to mastering the art of running a successful business. However, by staying committed and constantly seeking improvement using the concept of Kaizen, I overcame these obstacles.

Let's break down each stage, 1–7, so that you can understand how to bridge the gap between them. Each stage represents a significant milestone in your IT career, and achieving each one will bring you closer to your ultimate goal. Your IT journey will be unique and may look different from mine or any other student's journey. However, this guide will provide strong direction on what to do at each step so you never feel stuck and so you can continue to advance in your IT career in an accelerated manner. Whether you are just starting out without zero prior experience or are already an experienced IT professional, these insights will help you achieve greater success and satisfaction in your career that you might thought was never possible. Let's get started!

Stage 1: The Foundation (The Beginning: Humble Origins)

I truly believe that once you learn networking, it opens the gateway to all possibilities in information technology. The following diagram shows you what's possible once you have a strong foundation of IT principles and networking concepts.

Building this foundation requires two steps:

1. **Enhance your education and obtain relevant certifications.** I invested time and money into courses that aligned with my career goals. Gradually, I earned certifications in key areas such as:

CompTIA Network+ This certification helped me solidify my understanding of IT fundamentals and networking concepts.

Cisco Certified Network Associate (CCNA) This certification opened doors to more advanced networking roles and significantly boosted my technical skills.

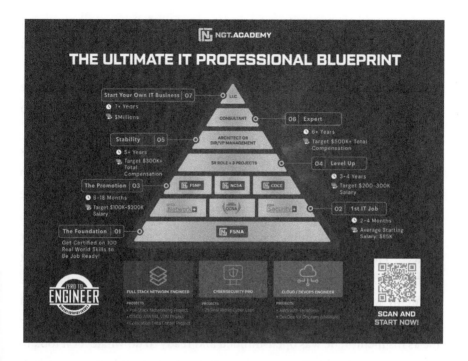

These certifications not only enhanced my résumé but also gave me the confidence and knowledge to take on more challenging roles. The process of studying and passing these exams taught me the value of discipline and perseverance.

2. Build a home lab or use simulators like Packet Tracer or GNS3 for hands-on training. You can set up a nice lab for a budget of around $1,000 or less.

Stage 2: First IT Job ($40,000–$80,000)

The goal at this stage is to break into the industry by joining an IT team. This is where a lot of people give up too easily. I remember hearing Ben Affleck and Matt Damon during an interview discussing how they would take any job with a crew when they first started in Hollywood just to get on a movie set where all the action is. It didn't matter if they were the errand boys getting coffee, holding up the camera stick, or taking out the garbage— they just wanted to get on the scene! This is how your mindset should be when starting in IT. Your only goal is to break into an existing IT team, no matter what. Get your foot in the door, and the rest will play out.

The best way to break into larger IT teams or Fortune 500 companies is to get an internship or offer to work for free. Another tactic is to hit up local businesses in your network; I suggest looking for companies that have at least 500 employees or more. The third option is to apply creatively to the open jobs posted online using LinkedIn and personal branding to get noticed. These tactics can all be used early in your career to get your foot in the door. For instance, one of the first 100 students I mentored in NGT Academy was Kevin Lee, who wanted to break into the tech industry but was unsure if he could make it without going back to college. By trusting me as his mentor, he was open-minded and ready to do whatever it took to accelerate fast. I said, "If you truly want to climb up this pyramid much faster, here's what you need to do."

He was a project manager for an art gallery in New York. I asked him if he was okay with getting paid minimum to zero for a 3-month internship. He said yes, since he was living with his parents and his bills were minimal. I said, "Great, here's what you need to do. Complete our Full Stack Network Associate (FSNA) training and obtain your CCNA," which he did in 60 days. After that, I told him to look up 10 Cisco Gold Partners, who are value-added resellers selling Cisco IT solutions to companies; contact the engineering manager or network engineer in the services delivery department; and arrange to meet as many of them as he could, saying that he aspired to be network engineer and wanted to get insights into their amazing company and how they operate.

My suggested strategy was to network and find a way in by asking each of the managers or engineer peers if he could volunteer for free on their infrastructure upgrade projects for their clients. It worked! After several meetings, he got his first yes: "We would love to have you as an intern and will even pay you!" So he took this paid internship for 2 months and then found a junior network engineer position at another reseller in town in month 3. Five months in, he secured his engineer position. After 2 years, he landed his dream job at Samsung. This was a student who also just immigrated to the United States during his freshman year, and English was his second language. The moral of the story is that if you get laser-focused and execute the plan to break in, then you can start to work your way up in the industry. Don't get caught up on the short-term sacrifice in pay or time, as once you secure the engineer title, your career is set for life as long as you keep up with industry trends and technologies—which will get easier to absorb over time once you go from beginner to SME in your career.

As you know, my journey began in a small IT support role where I was earning just $28,000 a year in 2005 at a local credit union. At that time, I was struggling to make ends meet and knew I couldn't survive off this salary for long to support my family of four. But I knew I was in the right career field; I just needed to move up the ranks and get laser-focused on securing the engineer title first. You see, most jobs have a ceiling, whereas network engineers who stay in the same profession for years or even decades enjoy salary increases. You see, it's not about how smart you are or how much potential you have; if you pick the wrong career, you will hit a ceiling, and in IT there is no such ceiling. It's really limitless on how much you can earn.

So, within 6 months, I went from network tech to network admin and received a pay raise to $60,000. A lot of folks now stop or stay stuck at this stage for years while earning $40,000–$80,000, just waiting for their yearly bonus or for when the boss gives them a promotion, which may or may not happen. This is a rookie mistake. You need to work on the next leg up within the next 12 months, as IT has limitless opportunities for those willing to master the advanced skills that pay the big bucks, which come in at Stage 3 and higher.

Stage 3: The Promotion ($80,000–$120,000)

At this stage we are solely focused on securing the engineer title in our job. Why? Because the average salary and market rate for engineers gets you to a higher income bracket. It's plain and simple; you can get paid two or three times more than entry-level jobs once you secure this title, giving you a pay range of $80,000–$120,000. (See Chapter 9, "Four More Steps to Demand Six-Figure Job Offers from Fortune 500 Companies," and check out the "Ten Strategies for Getting Promoted Quickly" sidebar.)

The main secret here is that you need to get exposed to IT projects running within your department. Ask for the IT budget planned for the year and see how you can get involved. At this stage your goal is to get more responsibility on your plate and start building some high-demand, mission-critical skills to support your employer. You see, while your peers are trying to get away with doing the minimum for their paychecks, you are being hungry, curious, and ambitious to learn new high-demand skills that are tied to big-budget IT projects. This is the stage in which you want to be able to participate and eventually lead your own IT projects. Once you have several projects under your belt, the promotion becomes easy and smooth.

In my case, I started searching for other jobs, lined up a few, and then had a discussion with my VP of IT at the time, when it became apparent he didn't want to lose me. Why? Because I'd been crucial to helping upgrade a lot of the IT infrastructure and replacing me would've cost much more than it would to give me a pay raise to low six figures. I got promoted to a position with a $102,000 salary within 12 months and I was able to secure the senior network engineer title. This was a game changer for me; once I secured the engineer title and broke six figures in salary, everything changed.

What I didn't expect to happen was the limitless opportunities that opened up for me. I learned there were even higher-level engineers who made two or four times more than my $102,000 salary, which was mind-blowing. Imagine after you secured a $40,000 entry-level IT job you learned you could increase your income 10 times over the next few years—would you believe it?

There are always levels to move up; you just need the courage and confidence to pursue learning the necessary skills as you move up.

Stage 4: Level Up with Projects ($120,000–$180,000)

I stayed in the senior network engineer role for 3 years, leading numerous IT projects with seven-figure budgets. I rolled out two data centers, upgraded IT infrastructure across 17 locations, and configured a full disaster recovery and business continuity plan using satellites in case AT&T had another major outage across the Gulf Coast.

This is the secret to my success and that of thousands of our students at NGT Academy. Why? Because we focus our training on these same concepts. For example, students in our Full Stack Network Engineering program get to architect, design, configure, implement, and finalize an entire infrastructure. This includes switches, routers, firewalls, VoIP and video systems, wireless, and secure remote access systems for an enterprise with a headquarters and two remote branches.

Mastering these high-demand skills for IT infrastructure upgrades allowed one student, Keron Taylor, to impress his technical hiring manager and secure a job at Google as a network engineer. He achieved this even without a college degree or industry certifications, simply due to his competency and ability to plan, design, and roll out infrastructure upgrades.

The following diagram illustrates the network infrastructure project Keron developed at NGT Academy, which played a key role in securing his job.

Network Topology

So remember, try to gain as much experience as possible working on IT projects during this phase. It's like an artist building a portfolio of work to showcase throughout their career. This is why I emphasize highlighting key IT projects on your résumé to stand out from the crowd. You can use the Résumé Template found in Appendix B.

Stage 5: Stability—Architect/ Director/VP Level ($180,000–$250,000)

At this stage, you've been implementing this blueprint for 3–5 years and have several IT projects in your portfolio that you can showcase. This is also a crucial stage where you can decide to stay on the technical path in your career or switch to managing a team within the IT department. In some cases, you may have already decided to move up to a director or VP level position, overseeing the entire department. Congratulations!

It took me 5 years to reach this stage, when I was recruited by Cisco Systems for a systems engineer position. I was customer-facing, creating IT solutions for some of Cisco's biggest clients on the Gulf Coast. At this point, you will have limitless options because you now have in-demand skills to understand new IT trends, quickly grasp technology, and design IT solutions to solve business problems. I call this the stage of stability because you are set for life. You can stay here and retire comfortably with a stable, high-demand job and complete job security. Just remember that to reach this stage you will want to go work for a tech manufacturer like Cisco, Amazon, Palo Alto Networks, Dell, Splunk, or Zoom, or at a reseller who sells these solutions (value-added resellers [VARs]). I call the tech companies the major leagues and the resellers the minor leagues. This is you jumping from the customer side to the client/consulting side of the house, which pays the big bucks! My recommendation is always to get to Stage 5 and try to join the major leagues, as I did working for Cisco Systems and Arista Networks in my career. Both are amazing companies; I could have simply retired if I hadn't decided to pursue starting my own business.

If you still want to move up the ranks, you could turn your years of working on IT projects into a consulting career. This could once again double your income, but keep in mind that the next step is not for everyone. There's nothing wrong with staying at the $180,000–$250,000 level as long as you love what you do!

Stage 6: Stability—Expert Consultant ($250,000–$500,000)

At this stage of my career, I got burnt out being a systems engineer/architect doing the same projects over and over again. I wanted to step into a consulting role, and that is when I joined Arista Networks. Arista was competing with Cisco Systems and taking market share away from them with innovative data center switching technologies that powered the data centers for eBay, Amazon, Facebook, and many more of the top giants in Silicon Valley. At Arista, I was able to secure the job title of technical account manager with a six-figure salary and the ability to earn hundreds of thousands of dollars in commissions. I was in charge of a big territory in Atlanta, and I was super excited about this role due to its potential to earn up to $500,000 or even higher.

This is the stage where you can also start your own consulting practice. In fact, this is the stage where the instructor for our Cloud/DevOps Engineering program went from earning $10,000 monthly to $40,000 monthly by becoming a consultant and eventually starting his own consulting business.

Stage 7: Start Your Own IT Business

At this stage I was already 15 years into my career and wanted to break out. In fact, I had done this twice—once in 2013 at the peak of my career at Cisco Systems earning $200,000, I thought "Is this it?" Then I got the start-up/entrepreneur bug, and I quit my corporate job to build a start-up and get venture backing. For two years, with four co-founders, we started CheckAction, a cloud-based project management app for IT teams. The concept was great, but learning how to launch, scale, and grow our own IT software business was scary and daunting. But I decided to jump ship anyway and so I did. After two years, the start-up had massively failed, but we did get into the Atlanta Tech Village's incubator and received $120,000 in funding. We were the first start-up to be accepted into their program. But eventually we ran out of cash, and I had to go back into the corporate world. But due to my high-demand IT project management and engineering skills, I was able to get multiple six-figure job offers from companies within a couple of months. However, after two years in the field again, while at Arista Networks, I got this burning desire to impact the education system and change the world!

This is when the idea of Zero to Engineer came about. I knew the college education system was broken because all my clients from Cisco and Arista Networks would tell me how bad they needed some competent engineers and that the college applicants were often incompetent and lacked hands-on experience. Plus, given that I'd trained thousands of young flight personnel as a technical instructor on Keesler Air Force Base with a top-secret clearance, I knew that it was possible to train people in months to support mission-critical networks and cybersecurity operations. This is the framework we've implemented with our job readiness training modules inside NGT Academy, paired with capstone IT projects that get people job ready as an engineer in 4 months and not 4 years. Colleges do not create the curriculum for you to be job ready—courses are mainly based on concepts, theories, and memorizations, whereas I knew from experience and having worked in the field for 15+ years that you truly level up through hands-on training and mentorship.

The year was 2016, and a for-profit college named ITT Tech Institute was shut down by the government education department, leaving 43,000 students stranded. This was bound to happen due to the false promises these types of colleges advertise in their late-night commercials charging students $85,000 for a network or cyber bachelor's degree. I'd thought this was a scam as I knew there was a faster, cheaper, efficient way to learn and gain hands-on skills training. This is when NGT Academy was born, and the rest is history.

Fast-forward nine years in building and changing lives every day at NGT Academy . . . People are starting to see the truth. The truth is you don't need to go to college to be successful in tech, and you sure don't need to pay some college $85,000 to flip a coin to see if you get a job after 4 years. This is why I started NGT Academy—to provide every American who wants to switch careers to information technology to be able to do so in months and not years, and do it cheaper, faster, and more efficiently than any college or university could. The choice is yours: 4 months or 4 years?

CONCLUSION

"The man who thinks he can and the man who thinks he can't are both right."

— Henry Ford

My journey from $28,000 to over $350,000 is a testament to the power of the Ultimate IT Professional Blueprint. By following its principles and strategies, I was able to transform my career and build a successful business from the ground up. I hope my story inspires you to take charge of your own career and achieve your dreams. Remember, with the right mindset, clear goals, continuous learning using Kaizen principles, and perseverance, anything is possible!

The Zero to Engineer movement is here to stay. Will you join us?

CHAPTER TWELVE

STUDENT SUCCESS STORIES

"You miss 100% of the shots you don't take."

— Wayne Gretzky

INTRODUCTION

I want to give you just a few super powerful success stories of NGT graduates that show what dedication, a strong foundation, and focused training can give you in the IT ecosystem. These stories, diverse as they are, underscore a common thread: Achieving personal and professional goals hinges not on where you start from, but on what decisions you make to get there. With the right mindset and support, anyone can break into this dynamic field.

Each story shows you how all the concepts and strategies we've discussed translate into getting that six-figure salary . . . and beyond! These students are the real-world examples of people just like you, so take this opportunity to reflect on your own path and identify what resonates with you.

As I've shown, it doesn't take 4 years of college and a fancy degree, but just 4 months of dedication, hands-on training, mentorship, and the right projects and labs to build the competency to get you job-ready to start your career.

The path from Zero to Engineer is not one you take alone. NGT Academy is here for you. We've trained thousands of students, taking them from Zero to Engineer. Jacob Hess, my cofounder and I, have trained thousands IT engineers as civilians and for the U.S. military, both holding Top Secret clearances and working in the IT career field for over 40 years combined. For our military students, we taught them to go from Zero to Engineer in just 16 weeks. So, yes, you can do it too.

At NGT Academy, we've taken everything in this book and condensed it into a 16-week program. By having this book, you are lightyears ahead of the curve, but only you can decide how quickly you get it done.

SUCCESS STORIES

Here are some stories that I hope will inspire you to take the leap of faith to build an amazing career for yourself, your family, and your loved ones. When you do, you'll reach financial freedom by working on the latest technologies and finding the ones that you're truly passionate about.

Kevin Lee

Before: Art Gallery Manager
After: Network Engineer

I want to start with Kevin Lee, who was in one of our first programs.

Kevin joined NGT Academy in the first year we launched our training school. I remember Kevin distinctly because, like me, he is a Korean

American and a first-generation immigrant who migrated to the United States in high school. His English was rather poor with a heavy accent, and he was working in New York as a project manager for an art gallery. Despite having student loan debt and a college degree, he didn't want to return to college. He joined our program with little knowledge about the industry but with a burning desire to break into technology. With these language and financial challenges, I want to share with you that if Kevin could make it, you too can go from Zero to Engineer by following the blueprint.

Kevin Lee completed our program in under 90 days. He secured a paid internship making $15 an hour, and after two months, landed an associate network engineer position. He achieved this title within five months of starting his career from scratch and earned $45,000 per year.

Now, fast-forward: One year later, he scored his dream job at Samsung, pulling in six figures in record time! That's Kevin Lee's story, but it could also be yours. Fast-forward again, five-plus years later, and he's managing Samsung's Wide Area Infrastructure team.

Chase Mitchell

Before: Unemployed
After: DevOps Engineer

Next up is Chase Mitchell. Chase stumbled upon one of our Zero to Engineer ads while he was in the hospital, laid off and unemployed. Before that, he was a campaign manager for a politician in Texas. Saddled with tens of thousands of dollars in student loan debt and holding a bachelor's degree in IT, Chase couldn't seem to break into the industry. He lacked confidence and hands-on training and had all but given up on his IT career. But after joining our program, within five months, we helped him secure a Cisco analyst position, earning

$40,000 a year. Just 11 months later, he was promoted to a data center network engineer position, raking in $90,000 and achieving one of his major goals—working from home. Fast-forward three years, and Chase landed his dream job at Amazon as a DevOps engineer!

Makeia Jackson

Before: Stay-at-Home Mom
After: Cybersecurity Technician

Makeia's story is a powerful testament to the transformative potential of our program. Despite a long-standing aspiration to become a cybersecurity professional, she continually dismissed it as an unrealistic goal. Not only did she feel it would cost too much, but as a stay-at-home mom, she did not feel she had the ability to attend classes.

She had a personal epiphany during the COVID-19 lockdown. Makeia found herself grappling with a sense of unfulfillment and isolation and decided it was time to make a change. She enrolled in our comprehensive training program and embarked on an extraordinary journey of professional development.

In a remarkably short span of just seven months, she successfully transitioned from being an unemployed stay-at-home parent to becoming a highly skilled cybersecurity specialist. The culmination of her hard work and determination was the attainment of an impressive $72,000 annual salary in her very first job within the industry.

Makeia's story exemplifies the empowering impact of accessible training with accelerated training pathways demonstrating how this program can profoundly change the lives of anyone with nerve, grit, and tenacity who want to strive to reach their full potential.

Chris Mendez

Before: IT Support Specialist
After: Network Engineer

Chris Mendez's journey from a frustrating entry-level IT role to a fulfilling career is an inspiring one. His story resonates with many trapped in positions that don't align with their aspirations or utilize their full potential.

When Chris joined our program, he was working in a role that left him feeling unfulfilled and anxious. His days were filled with mundane tasks and constant firefighting, dealing with a variety of issues from server problems to printer malfunctions. The relentless cycle of putting out fires created a high-stress environment that was taking its toll on his well-being.

Chris felt stuck in this position for years until he found our program. We helped him transition to a network engineer position within six months, and he received a massive 50 percent salary increase right out of the gate.

After attending one of our programs, Chris's career was remarkable. He successfully transitioned from his entry-level job to a position as a network engineer. The career leap not only provided Chris with more challenging and fulfilling work but also came with a substantial salary increase.

Today, he enjoys working as a network specialist supporting a large metropolitan city in California. He has not only improved his professional life but also his overall well-being.

Keron Taylor

Before: Chemical Operator
After: Network Engineer

Let's talk about Keron Taylor, whose story is nothing short of incredible. Keron was working as a forklift driver in a chemical plant. He had dropped out of college, frustrated by the lack of hands-on learning, and was shouldering around $25,000 in student loans. He knew that college didn't help with his learning style, as he needed practical, hands-on experience. Keron had almost given up on his IT aspirations until a turning point—he saw his friend, a fellow forklift driver, get laid off because an automated robot replaced him. It hit him like a ton of bricks; technology was advancing so quickly that it literally took his friend's job. He realized he needed to dive into the tech world immediately.

We guided Keron through NGT Academy, and within five months, he secured a position as a data center operations engineer. His enthusiasm was infectious, and I remember telling him that this was just the beginning. When I asked him about his dream job, he said it was to work for Google. We set that as a goal for the next 12 months. But guess what? Within just six months, Keron's competence and experience impressed a Google manager so much during an interview that he got a job offer on the spot to join as a network engineer—no college degree required. Three years later, Keron is now managing the network engineering team at Google. Truly an awe-inspiring story!

Keron's motivation stemmed from his wakeup call—those pivotal moments in life that compel us to act. My wakeup call was Hurricane Katrina, which left me unemployed and tasked with supporting my family of four. Keron had to care for his family of five when he found himself unemployed due to a work injury and seeing his friend replaced by automation.

So, what's your wakeup call? Life changes pivot on two things: desperation or inspiration. Whether your back is against the wall or you're fueled by the stories you're reading, I urge you to make your choice. Know that if Keron could do it, you can too.

Andy Pratt

Before: Network Administrator
After: Systems Engineer

Next is Andy Pratt. Andy was actually already in IT as a network administrator. As I've mentioned, people get stuck in these entry-level roles where they're not making much money. In Andy's case, even though he was a U.S. Air Force veteran, he was stuck at $50,000 for a few years. But with a family of four, he knew something had to change.

I helped coach and mentor Andy with our program and got him to $90,000 within just three months using the same blueprint you have been given in this book. By working on getting a promotion using Step 2 from Chapter 8 he was able to get a 50 percent pay bump within 90 days and landed a full-time contract position at NASA as a network engineer, using Step 5 from Chapter 8 and securing that engineer job title.

It was as simple as having to work on getting away from the network admin title and securing the engineer title. That's what we helped him do in just 90 days. And then, 10 months later, Andy broke into a systems engineer role, earning over $150,000 working for Riot Games, where he could work from home five days a week.

This was a huge goal of his because his spouse was active-duty military, so he needed to be able to move around if she was stationed somewhere else. He still works at Riot Games, but his dreams have come true, and he's blown past $200,000 as a systems engineer.

Karl Scott

Before: Bicycle Delivery in New York
After: Cybersecurity Analyst
Consultant

For almost 10 years, Karl struggled in the user and digital experience field. He found himself, at 60 years old, running errands on a bike in New York City, earning about $15 per hour and working any freelance web development job he could find.

After connecting with NGT, Karl leveraged the Zero to Engineer blueprint to transform his life. Within nine months, he started working for Accenture, a top-tier consulting company. His starting salary was over $101,000, going from Zero to Engineer with a six-figure starting salary right out the gate! If he can do it, so can you.

Jon Mallory

Before: Pharmaceutical Researcher
After: Network Security Engineer

I'd like to introduce Jon Mallory, a 31-year-old resident of Nashville, Tennessee. Jon now proudly holds the position of a network security engineer with CDW Corp. But the journey to this point in his life was far from easy.

Jon's older brother Jeffrey is on the autism spectrum. This condition presents various social challenges, which unfortunately led Jeffrey to become a victim of an IRS phone scam a few years ago. Jeffrey lost thousands of dollars in this scam, and this incident deeply affected Jon. He was upset and angry. It spurred him on to delve into the world of cybersecurity, hoping to combat such instances of fraud and identity theft.

Before this, Jon was employed in a drug testing lab in Nashville, a job that did not fulfill him. He believed there was more he could achieve. After some research, he discovered the vast realm of cybersecurity careers, but he was unsure of which path to pursue.

As fate would have it, while browsing Instagram after one day at work, he stumbled upon an ad featuring Jacob Hess's welcoming face, promoting an NGT course. Intrigued, Jon delved deeper, realizing that our platform was professional and that we genuinely cared about our teaching.

Jon decided to join the course, appreciating the structured approach and, above all, the continuous support provided throughout the program. The mentors were a lifeline for him. He worked with the NGT team for a year when an exciting opportunity presented itself. The Career Services department informed him about the launch of a new cybersecurity program.

At the same time, a job opportunity in a data center surfaced. After a moment of consideration, Jon decided to pursue both opportunities, understanding that the data center job would offer hands-on experience, complementing his recent cybersecurity learning.

Jon landed his first IT job with IES Communications at the data center, and he stayed there for almost a year until Bobby from NGT Academy presented him with an incredible opportunity at CWS. John seized the opportunity.

He was offered a position in network security, a field he had prepared for with his recent certifications. Securing the job brought him more fulfillment than he ever dreamed. The prospect of working remotely, avoiding the commute into Nashville every day, made it even better.

The new job not only presented a fulfilling career but also led to a huge salary hike. Jon's income increased by 100 percent from his healthcare job and 50 percent from the data center position. The financial stability allowed him to clear debts, upgrade his vehicle, and even save for a down payment on a house.

Joe Cabezuela

Before: U.S. Army Officer
After: Network Engineer

Meet Joe, a man deeply passionate about his work in IT. For him, the first IT job was all about proving himself, demonstrating his knowledge and making a mark. After graduating with a bachelor's degree in technical communication, Joe felt ready to enter the IT industry. However, he soon realized the field required more practical experience and certifications. Following graduation, Joe enlisted in the U.S. Army, searching for a clean, technical role that offered a sense of community and purpose.

After a decade in service, the long, grueling hours began to take a toll on him. When he was notified he'd be given a medical retirement, it came as a blow. But Joe saw the silver lining. If he couldn't serve actively, he could still contribute as a civilian, perhaps as a network engineer for a contractor or a Department of Defense employee.

This is when NGT Academy came into the picture. Joe got in touch with us, did his due diligence, and his decision was met with complete support from his Army chain of command and his spouse. Together they understood that our program was a stepping stone to a promising civilian life after the military. The program helped Joe catch up on past skills and learn new ones for the future, reinforcing his confidence and self-assurance.

After graduation, Joe realized how much the program's projects and network upgrades mirrored his current work. When in doubt, he would refer to NGT program labs, revisit lesson plans, and brush up his skills to tackle real-world troubleshooting issues.

He made it clear that NGT Academy's confidence in its students, our job placement support, and especially the mock interview sessions were immensely helpful. Joe found himself in a better place in life, primarily working from home, traveling occasionally, and, most importantly, doing what he loved.

His wife shared that the completion of the program was a turning point for Joe. It resulted in multiple job offers that allowed him to work from home. Now, the couple didn't have to worry about military drills or deployments, having more time to relax and enjoy their life together.

In Joe's words, "Thanks to NGT Academy, I'm working a job as a network engineer that allows me to spend more time with my family while at the same time get to travel and grow in my position."

Iris Colon

Before: Insurance Sales
After: NOC Technician

"I went into NGT at a literal zero, and I knew absolutely nothing. And now, thanks to NGT, I found my niche in the job market."

— Iris Colon

Iris Colon went from selling insurance to working as a network operations center (NOC) technician. She had zero knowledge about technology when she joined NGT, a life-changing opportunity she found while scrolling Facebook. Unsatisfied with her career in insurance sales, Iris always had an interest in technology. She loved setting up her home network and other similar tasks. It was her affinity for technology that led her to click on our NGT ad.

The program became a gateway to a new life. One day, Iris received an email from a company that had come across her profile on LinkedIn. They asked if she was still looking for a job and offered her a position as an NOC technician. The job interview went well, and she landed the position. On her first day on the job, Iris's competence made an impression. Her new colleagues noted that she answered questions in a way many senior engineers wouldn't have been able to.

None of this would have been possible without NGT, from teaching her essential skills to preparing her to shine in the interview. We provided her with the knowledge she needed and the confidence to pursue a career in a field she had always been passionate about.

Travis Sanchez

Before: Food Server
After: Network Administrator

At just 18 years old, Travis Sanchez went from slinging spaghetti to building networks. Before joining, he faced the daily grind of a 35-minute commute to his job as a waiter, where he earned just below California's average of $16 an hour.

With the impending burden of attending college looming, Travis was feeling overwhelmed by the cost of tuition at this local community college, which is estimated at the lower end at $54,000 for an associate's degree. He was on the cusp of completing his enrollment when he heard about NGT Academy.

His discovery of NGT proved to be a game changer. Travis found the academy's 4-month program much more appealing than the traditional college path. He joined NGT in August 2023 and finished the Full Stack Network Associate level of the program by September of that year and his CCNA one month later. By January he secured a help desk job, and following the career path advice provided by NGT, soon advanced to a network administrator role. Not only did Travis make his career choice in months instead of years, but he now enjoys an average starting salary of $74,000—a significant leap from his earnings in the food service industry.

Tricia Sanchez

Before: Unemployed
After: IT Project Manager

Let me introduce you to Tricia. Tricia is nothing short of a hard worker and has been that way her entire life. Growing up on a farm, she was used to the daily physical and mental challenges that were pressed upon her. This helped shape her work ethic moving into her adult life.

Prior to NGT in her adult life, she was a classically trained musician and educated with a master's in fine arts. She worked over a decade in the events planning space primarily in the entertainment industry, working her way up to events services director, handling live concerts and events. Just like many people, COVID hit her industry hard, and her job basically vanished overnight. She had some ups and downs in her field the next couple years but eventually decided she needed to make a change to a more reliable career path. That's when she found NGT.

Although she didn't have an IT background, Tricia was no stranger to hard work. She started out with a bang in training and was able to land her first role as an IT project manager soon after gaining her Security+ certification with us. This role is an excellent starting point into IT for her and a way to leverage skills gained in training and in her past career. As expected, she continues to train with NGT, on her own and on the job to continue growing in her career.

Jason Hoang

Before: Private Tutor
After: Wireless Consulting Engineer

Our next student, Jason, is a great example of growth in the industry. He came to NGT as a private tutor for math and science. Just like many teachers, he wasn't making nearly enough money in the education field.

Jason is very proactive and started studying in IT on his own, reading the Cisco CCNA book and studying for the Network+ certification. He realized quickly that he was missing the hands-on experience that would be needed for the field. As a beginner with no IT experience, he was drawn to NGT because of our training methodology that focuses on skills training to prepare you for the job, just like Terry did in the military.

Jason studied hard and graduated from NGT with hands-on training and his CCNA certification. He soon was able to land his first IT role at CDW working as a wireless associate consulting engineer, doubling his previous salary. Through hard work and continuing education, he was able to land a promotion to wireless consulting engineer and brought his salary over the six-figure threshold, all within two years. He's direct proof that training with a plan will get you to your goals!

Roshode McQueen

Before: Car Dealership Report Auditing
After: PCI DSS Cybersecurity

With us from the beginning, Roshode joined NGT Academy in 2020. A distinguished Navy veteran, he obtained an NGT Cyber Security Associate certificate in four months. His first job after he transitioned from the military was in governance, risk, and compliance (GRC), but he found himself stuck in his career, only finding general risk analysis jobs afterward. In Texas, the average salary for this position is $77,520.

After obtaining his NGT Academy certification, he quickly landed a job at Wipro as a GRC specialist. Through dedication, he progressed in his career to his current position as a PCI DSS cybersecurity consultant, working remotely for a well-known cybersecurity consulting firm whose average salary for a consultant is $109,000.

In a student feedback survey, Roshode shared these encouraging words: "Keep progressing and helping the way that you do."

Dionne Davis

Before: Vendor Analyst
After: IT Specialist

Dionne's story is a great example of the power of grit and determination. In 2021, she joined NGT Academy's part-time cyber cohort class, which she completed in two months. However, her journey to securing employment was not without its challenges. As a job seeker in the highly competitive DMV (DC, Maryland, and Virginia) region, Dionne initially struggled to find a suitable position largely due to the prevalent requirement for security clearance in the area. Undeterred, Dionne proactively sought the guidance of a career success coach. Through this collaborative effort, Dionne was able to land a role as a network analyst, even though it required a longer commute than she had initially preferred. Recognizing the value of this opportunity to advance her career, Dionne was willing to put in the necessary time and effort, and her perseverance paid off tremendously.

Today, Dionne's hard work has culminated in an exceptional achievement—she now holds the position of IT specialist with the United States Department of Defense. This role boasts an impressive average base salary of $83,000 per year, underscoring the significant career growth and financial rewards that Dionne has attained through her unwavering commitment and resilience. Dionne's story serves as a powerful testament to the transformative impact of grit and determination. By embracing challenges, leveraging available resources, and maintaining a steadfast focus on her professional goals, she has successfully navigated the competitive job market and secured a remarkable career opportunity that aligns with her aspirations. Her success story is an inspiration to all who strive to overcome obstacles and achieve their dreams.

Craig Fowler

Before: Plumber
After: NOC Technician

Let me introduce you to Craig Fowler. This is a great story about a blue-collar worker making the transition to his dream career. He was working as a plumber by trade. He knew he wanted to make a change in his career and had concocted a plan to do that. Craig was enrolled in a university for almost four years, working on a degree toward IT, when he realized he needed help and college wasn't giving him the skills that he needed.

He found NGT online and pivoted toward our expedited learning approach. Craig focused on specializing in a career in networking and came in with a goal to break into the field. Very quickly he realized he was in the right place based on the quality of training he was receiving. He even mentioned that he learned more in six months at NGT than the entire time he was in college. Wow!

On his first call with a career adviser he said his five-year goal was to become a senior network engineer. Upon graduation, Craig was able to quickly land his first IT role working as a network operations center technician at Think Tank NTG. He gained some excellent experience and has since moved up to a network engineer role, well on his way of achieving his five-year goal. We are looking forward to seeing many more years of growth for Craig's career.

Richard Gan

Before: Property Management
After: Data Center Technician

Meet Richard, an excellent example of taking his life into his own hands and changing his life trajectory. For many years, Richard was working in property management and didn't see a way to grow in his current field. As a kid, he grew up around technology because of his dad and always had engineering in the back of his mind as an adult.

The turning point in Richard's life was when he decided to take the leap of faith and enrolled with NGT Academy in March 2024. Within a month, he gained his first certification through NGT, the Full Stack Network Associate (FSNA) certification. This gave him the groundwork to build and grow into his new career.

Immediately after gaining the FSNA, he started his job hunt. Working closely with the NGT Career Services team, he was able to revamp his marketability and focus on preparing for these technical interviews. Through this process, he landed his first job as a data center technician at MacStadium, approximately two months after he started training. It's truly amazing what Richard was able to achieve and shows how staying disciplined in your studies can help you reach your goals in record time.

Rodrigo Ramos

Before: Public Servant
After: Cybersecurity Consultant

Rodrigo Ramos had a career as a public servant in Mexico City, focusing on security. Politically motivated firings are sadly getting more prevalent in Mexico, and he was unable to thrive. He decided to leverage his security background with portable IT skills that will allow him stability and growth.

He considered enrolling in MIT before he heard about NGT Academy. Between the difference in the tuition and time frame, he chose NGT. In three months he completed the NCSA program and is now *consultor de ciberseguridad* (a cybersecurity consultant). The typical salary for this position is MXN$225,000, but most importantly Rodrigo now has a career in which he can grow and thrive. *Asi se hace*, Rodrigo!

Anna Mensah

Before: Homemaker
After: IT Security Analyst

Anna is a true diamond in the rough, whose radiant potential has been polished through her remarkable journey. Originally from Ghana, Anna faced the daunting task of reentering the workforce after a seven-year hiatus as a homemaker. Her determination and willingness to seek support propelled her forward as she enrolled in NGT Academy with hope.

Despite initial nervousness, Anna tackled challenges, completing her FSNA certification in just four months. Encouraged by her accomplishment, she successfully finished the program and earned her coveted

CCNA certification as well laying the foundation for her professional career.

Anna then landed a role as a third-party risk analyst, and she grew her career from there. Today, she proudly works as an IT security analyst at the Kellogg Company, earning over $77,000. A true Zero to Engineer success, Anna's story testifies to the transformative impact of affordable education and the value provided by NGT, shining brightly as the diamond she has become.

Stephen Philip

Before: Line Cook
After: IT Analyst

The fantastic journey of Stephen Philip starts in Nigeria and extends to Chicago and then to NGT Academy. Stephen worked as a line cook in a restaurant in a Marriott Hotel. Despite the time demands of his job, Stephen was determined to create a better life. He completed the first part of the NGT program in three months. Reflecting on his time there, he recalls the supportive environment, stating, "Once you have any kind of problem and you reach out to them, people are ready to respond."

Encouraged by his career coach, Stephen took a bold step and reached out to the IT department at Marriott. He shared his training and career aspirations, and his initiative paid off. Stephen was swiftly hired as an IT analyst, a role that came with a significant salary increase of $50,000.

Stephen's journey from line cook to IT analyst is not just a career progression; it is a story of personal growth and the realization of dreams. His experience at NGT Academy provided him with the skills and confidence to transform his life. Stephen's story is a heartwarming reminder that with the right support and determination, anyone can achieve their goals and create a brighter future for themselves.

Al Minnigan

Before: Technician
After: Level 2 Network
Security Admin

Al's journey is a familiar one for many aspiring IT professionals. After a decade as a technician for a school district, he found himself feeling stuck. The district's new initiative to provide every student with a laptop turned his role into a constant cycle of troubleshooting and frustration. What was once a fulfilling job had become monotonous, and his spouse noticed his increasing unhappiness when he came home each night.

Determined to change his situation, Al began studying for the Network+ certification on his own but struggled to make progress. It was then that he discovered NGT. After reaching out and discussing his goals with one of the career advisers, he realized that NGT's structured training program was exactly what he needed.

Al immersed himself in NGT's training, earning his Cisco CCNA and completing the Advanced Infrastructure projects in the FSNP section. These achievements boosted his confidence and reignited his passion for his career.

With newfound skills and confidence, Al took proactive steps at work, seeking out new projects and shadowing the infrastructure department. His eagerness and improved capabilities did not go unnoticed. When a Level 2 Network Security Admin position opened up, Al was encouraged to apply. Despite facing competition from 12 other internal candidates, he secured the role.

Al credits much of his success to the training and guidance he received from NGT. Beyond his professional growth, the positive mindset and self-assurance he gained have transformed other aspects of his life. He now demonstrates to his kids the importance of advocating for oneself and pursuing one's goals with determination.

Kwame Ohemeng

Before: Warehouse Worker
After: Network Engineer

Kwame's story is a remarkable testament to the power of perseverance and the American Dream. Born and raised in Ghana, Kwame worked diligently as an entry-level network specialist at a television network, all the while nurturing a dream to live in the United States. Like countless others, he applied for the visa lottery program, hoping for a chance to turn his dream into reality. By sheer luck, Kwame won the lottery and was awarded a resident visa to the United States.

Upon his arrival, Kwame faced the challenging reality of starting over. He had hoped to leverage his educational background and experience to quickly resume his career in IT. However, he soon discovered that his qualifications and experience didn't translate as smoothly as he had anticipated. Faced with the need to support himself, Kwame took a job in a warehouse, making ends meet while he sought new opportunities.

Determined not to let this setback deter him, Kwame began exploring resources online and stumbled upon NGT Academy. He was drawn to the academy's mentorship program and decided to enroll. Through intensive training and certification, Kwame updated his skills and benefited from the guidance of experienced mentors, including Terry, who played a pivotal role in his development.

Equipped with new qualifications and renewed confidence, Kwame set out to find a role in IT. His efforts soon paid off in an unexpected way: he was invited to join Cisco's prestigious "Dream Team" at Cisco Live, an exclusive event reserved for top students from across the United States and Canada. This opportunity provided Kwame with invaluable insights into building complex networks and reinforced his belief in his abilities.

Not long after Cisco Live, Kwame secured his first IT job as a network engineer. Over the years, his dedication and expertise earned him a reputation as the go-to expert in his department. His career flourished, and he eventually advanced to the position of senior network engineer.

Kwame's journey is a powerful example of how dreams, combined with determination and the right guidance, can lead to extraordinary achievements. His story is a celebration of resilience and the transformative impact of hard work and mentorship.

Brent Whited

Before: Cyber Analyst
After: Senior Cybersecurity Engineer

Brent's journey from serving our country to finding his dream career is inspiring. After dedicating years protecting our nation as a cyber defense operator in the U.S. Marines, Brent faced the challenge of transitioning to civilian life. He wanted to ensure that his military experience would translate in the private sector in a way that would qualify him for a position in which he could work remotely.

When Brent discovered NGT Academy, he was drawn to our reputation for excellence and focus on practical relevant skills. Brent saw the opportunity to be able to take his cybersecurity expertise to the next level.

Approaching his studies with the same discipline and dedication that served him well in the Marines, the academy's military-based hands-on approach resonated with his learning style, allowing him to progress through the program quickly, and he soon landed an information security position. But Brent's journey did not end there. Today he has achieved what many in the tech industry aspire to: a position as a senior cybersecurity engineer at T-Mobile, one of the nation's leading telecommunications companies—and he can work remotely.

Brent's story exemplifies our mission to provide practical, career-focused education that empowers students to achieve their goals and NGT Academy's goal of continuing to help aspiring IT professionals reach their potential.

Robert Hardy

Before: Musician, USMC
After: Level II IT Support Specialist

Robert's journey from musician and Marine to successful IT professional is a testament to his adaptability and the power of targeted education. His story is particularly inspiring as it showcases how one can overcome multiple career transitions and still find success in a new field.

After serving his country honorably in the U.S. Marines, Robert faced the daunting challenge of transitioning to civilian life. Like many veterans, he found himself at a crossroads, seeking a new career path that would leverage his skills and provide long-term stability.

Recognizing the growth opportunity in the tech industry, Robert decided to pivot his career to IT. He found his path forward with NGT Academy, liking the program known for its comprehensive and practical approach to IT education. The program's focus on hands-on, real-world applications proved to be the perfect fit for Robert's learning style.

The impact of the quality of his training became evident almost immediately. Upon completing the fundamentals program, he quickly secured a position at a well-known bio-pharmaceutical company with a starting salary of $68,000.

Robert's success story doesn't end with landing the job. He was able to make a significant impact. Drawing on his hands-on experience and troubleshooting methodology, he provided immediate value to his new employer. His ability to solve patching issues so early in his tenure not only validated his skills but also demonstrated the job-ready nature of the NGT Academy program.

For veterans and career changes alike, Robert's story serves as an inspiration. It demonstrates that regardless of your background, with the right education and mindset, you can quickly acquire the skills needed to thrive in the tech industry.

Logan Brindley

Before: Warehousing
After: System Administrator

Here's another compelling story about a student transitioning from a physically demanding blue-collar job to a career in IT. Logan was working in a warehouse, growing tired of the abuse his body was taking on a day-to-day basis and the late-night graveyard shifts he was working. Unsurprisingly, Logan pushed his body too far and sustained an injury at work. Not only was he out of work for a month, but his employer didn't acknowledge his injury as a qualifying worker's compensation claim. This was the spark he needed to really make a change.

This is when Logan found NGT. He liked what NGT was offering and it truly looked fun to him. He didn't wait for his luck to change; he took action to make it change. After Logan gained the skills he needed, he started browsing online for opportunities. Among those, he found a position for a programming role at eFusion, unrelated to his studies at NGT but something that always interested him. He wasn't fully qualified for it but was confident and wanted to interview anyway.

During the interview process with eFusion, the hiring manager was impressed with his knowledge after coming out of training and thought he'd be perfect for a systems engineering role. The problem was, they'd just filled that role a couple days prior.

As luck would have it, Logan received a call from the hiring manager three weeks later that the previous hire didn't work out and he wanted him to officially interview for the position. Of course, Logan was elated and came in the next week for an interview. As expected, he did great on his technical interview and was hired with a pay raise from his warehouse role.

Just like that, Logan's life completely changed. He's enjoying what he does in his daily life. He gets to sleep on a normal schedule. Most importantly, he gets to spend plenty of time with his family, which he was missing out on before. One of the most powerful things Logan mentioned in his interview with us was, "Because of NGT, I've not only been able to find a job I love, but I'm able to chart a course for my life going forward."

Nathan Nicely

Before: Fire Protection Industry
After: Network Support Analyst

Nate is a current NGT mentor, technical instructor, and network support analyst, but his story doesn't start there. Before everything Nate has achieved, he was working in the fire protection industry. He had essentially hit a ceiling at his current career in all aspects. He knew he didn't want to do this the rest of his life and wanted more out of a career.

When Nate started looking for a career in IT, he knew he wanted to get certifications but wasn't sure what path to take. Does he go back to college, read some books, or find another training option? That's when he discovered NGT, and our message really stuck with him. He scheduled a call with a career adviser and realized that he could gain the experience needed to reach his goals.

Nate jumped into training and began on the networking pathway. He was essentially starting from scratch. He followed the simplified pathway that Jacob lays out by following the FSNA training to gain the fundamentals, gained his CCNA certification, and focused on the advanced projects and labs. This training and structure just made sense to him. After gaining the skills, he was concerned about how to translate his knowledge to a résumé. This is where NGT Career Services helped him stand out and be marketable to potential employers. The layout of the projects piqued the interest of hiring managers and landed him his first interview.

As with most people, it can be a little intimidating going into an interview, especially for a field you never worked in. Nate reached out to one of the NGT Alumni and Mentors, Sergio Maldonado. They spent a couple hours going over interviewing strategies to prepare him for the upcoming interviews. Nate ended up going through two rounds of interviews in three days before he was offered the job. What he didn't expect was to be making $81,000 for an entry-level role in a completely new career field, a $20,000 bump from his prior career.

This entire process from start to finish took him eight months to completely change his life. He saved a ton of time and money while setting himself up for financial success in the future. These days you will still find Nate working in the networking field while being an active technical instructor and mentor for NGT students.

Junwon Suh

Before: Retail Sales Manager
After: Junior Penetration Tester

As a native Korean speaker, Junwon faced the dual challenge of not only changing careers but also navigating the technical complexities of cybersecurity in a non-native language. Recognizing the growing demand for IT professionals and his own passion for technology, Junwon made the bold decision to pivot his career. He found his path forward with NGT Academy. Despite the language barrier, Junwon's determination and the academy's supportive learning environment allowed him to thrive.

The impact of NGT Academy's training on his career has been profound. In his own words, "The courses have directly helped me in my role." Junwon's success story demonstrates it's possible to successfully transition into IT, regardless of your background or native language.

Today, Junwon is a successful penetration tester and contributing to the vital field of cybersecurity. His journey from sales manager to IT professional highlights the growing global demand for skilled cybersecurity experts. His story exemplifies our mission to provide practical, career-focused education that empowers students from all backgrounds to achieve their professional goals in the dynamic world of technology and cybersecurity.

CONCLUSION

For more inspiring stories like these, visit http://ZerotoEngineer .com/success-stories and witness countless individuals from various walks of life transforming their careers with our proven blueprint. I know these stories will propel you forward in your journey to become an IT rock star.

On our website, you will see that we have Network Engineering, Cybersecurity, Cloud, QA Automation, and Systems Engineering training programs, and we will continue to add tracks that have the most demand in the marketplace for years to come. Just visit https://ngt.academy or https://zerotoengineer.com to get started.

INDEX